Wakefield Press

CLAY GULLY

Sally van Gent lives in a forest near Bendigo with her husband and their many demanding dogs, fish, tame magpies and visiting kangaroos.

Sally was born in England, where she trained as a teacher at Bretton Hall College for Music, Art and Drama. She has lived in many countries, including Qatar, Abu Dhabi, Kuwait, Mauritius and Singapore, and has been a longtime birdwatcher and field naturalist. Sally survived breast cancer – helped, she believes, by her affinity with nature.

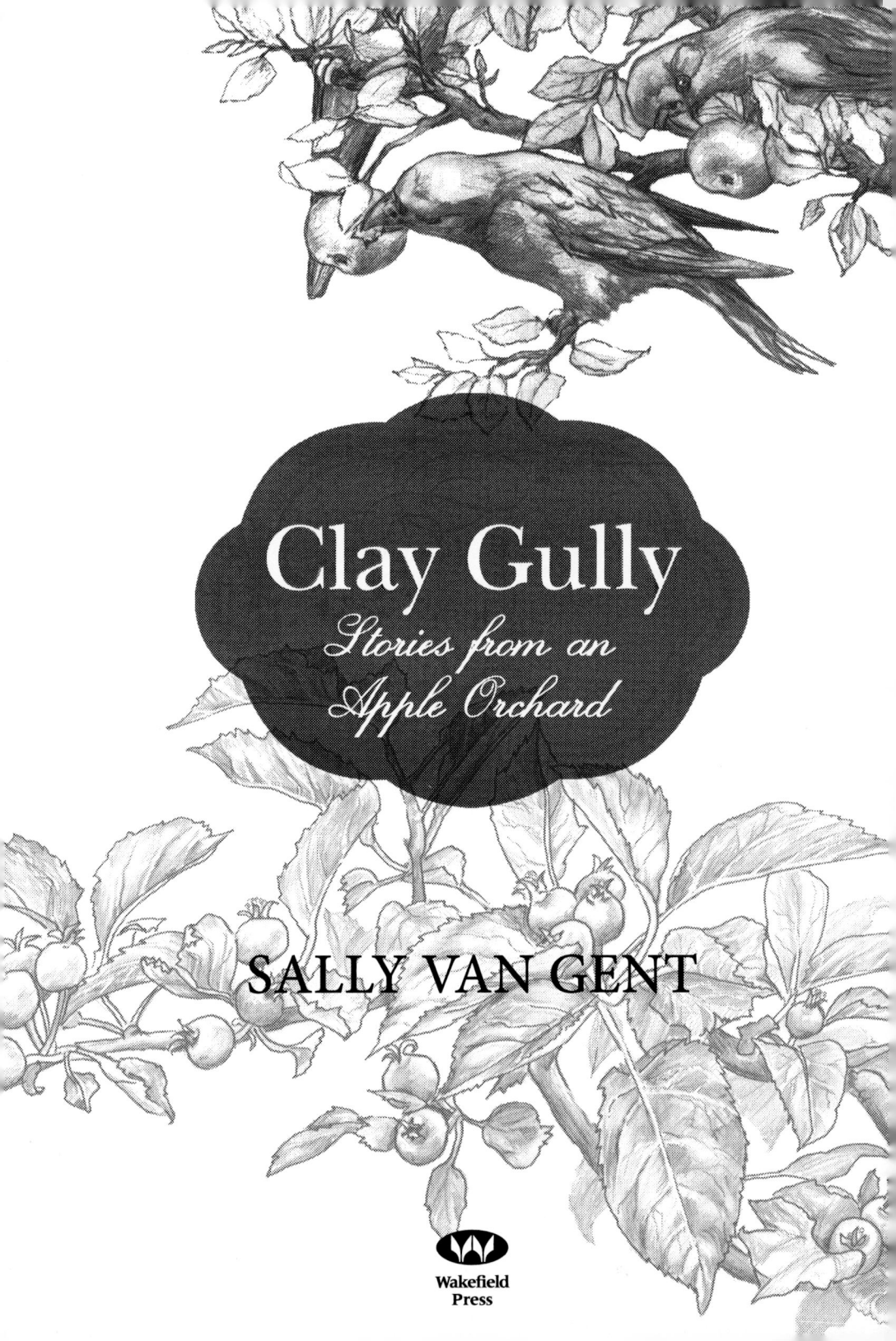

Clay Gully
Stories from an Apple Orchard

SALLY VAN GENT

Wakefield Press

Wakefield Press
1 The Parade West
Kent Town
South Australia 5067
www.wakefieldpress.com.au

First published 2013

Copyright © Sally van Gent, 2013

All rights reserved. This book is copyright. Apart from any fair dealing for the purposes of private study, research, criticism or review, as permitted under the Copyright Act, no part may be reproduced without written permission. Enquiries should be addressed to the publisher.

Edited by Julia Beaven, Wakefield Press
Cover designed by Stacey Zass, page 12
Illustrated and designed by Sally van Gent
Typeset by Clinton Ellicott, Wakefield Press
Printed and bound by Prestige Copying and Printing, Adelaide

National Library of Australia Cataloguing-in-Publication entry

Author:	Gent, Sally van.
Title:	Clay Gully: stories from an apple orchard / written and illustrated by Sally van Gent.
ISBN:	978 1 74305 188 7 (pbk.).
Subjects:	Gent, Sally van.
	Apple growers – Australia – Biography.
	Country life – Australia – Biography.
	Animals – Anecdotes.
Dewey Number:	634.11092

Publication of this book was assisted by the Commonwealth Government through the Australia Council, its arts funding and advisory body.

*For my grandchildren
Edward, Rose and Ari,
Ben and James.*

Contents

PART ONE

Turning the Soil

1

PART TWO

Bramleys, Bees and Button Quail

39

PART THREE

Drought

91

Acknowledgements   129

Recipe Index   131

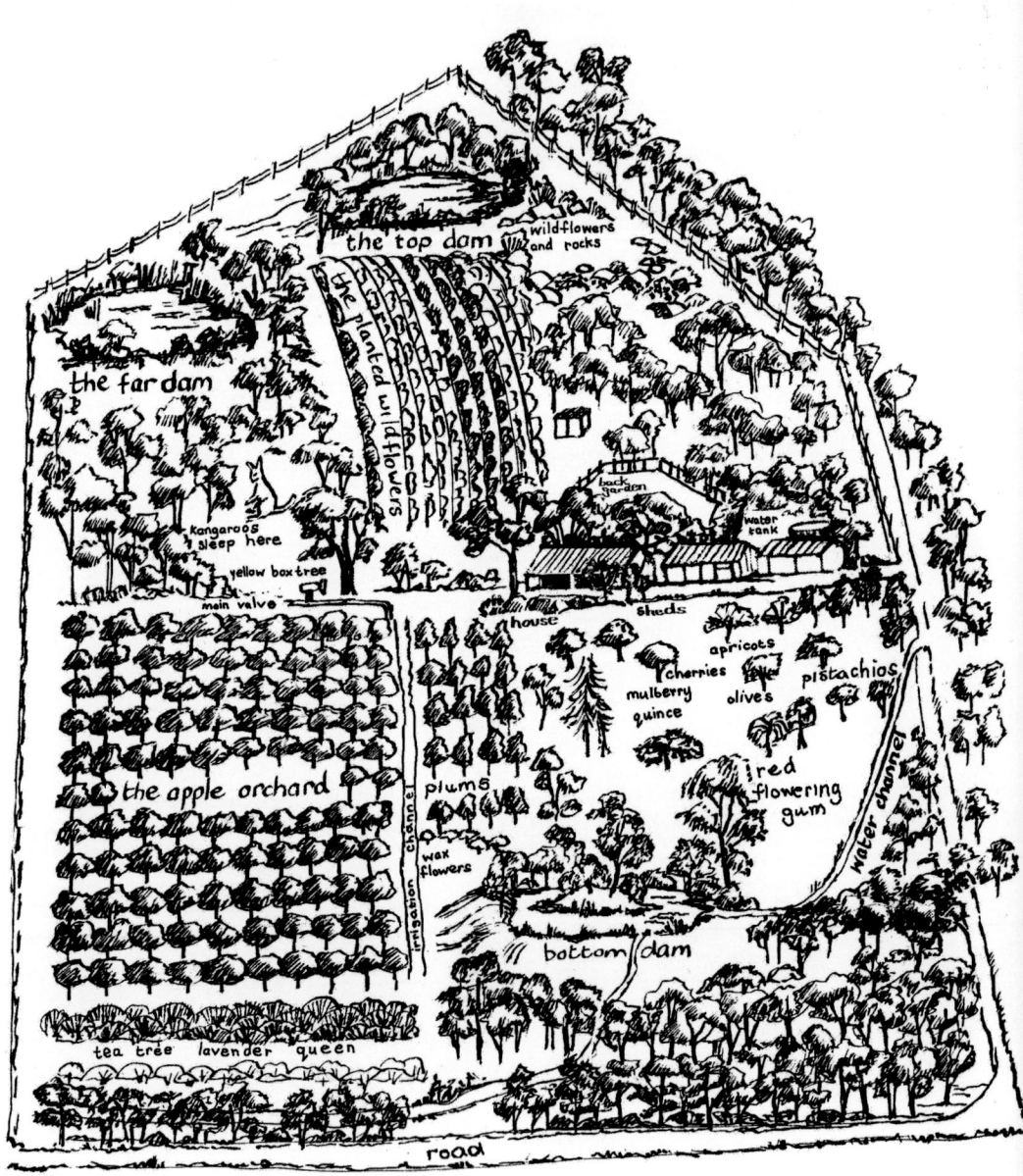

PART ONE

Turning the Soil

After several months of fruitless searching around Bendigo in central Victoria, the agent calls to tell us he has found our perfect home. Apparently the house is in the middle of ten acres of bush and farmland. Right away I know we can't afford a property like that. The agent insists I at least drive past the place.

He tells me, 'If you wait a bit the price will come down. I've heard the owners are about to go bankrupt.'

How would you like to pay this man to sell your house, I wonder.

Out of curiosity I drive down the winding dirt road. To the left are green paddocks where a horse is grazing. On the other side there is forest, all the way down the hill. At the bottom, where there is a wide curve in the road, I spot the house through the gum trees. It stands in the centre of a lightly treed paddock and to the side is open bush land. The agent persuades us to have a look inside. The house, though adequate, is unimpressive. It has a dingy seventies-style kitchen and worse, there is ghastly brown and cream shag-pile carpet almost everywhere. I look at the view through the living-room window and I don't care.

It's been a wet spring and water cascades over the paddocks, draining from the bush higher up the hill. The agent sends us off to walk around the property unaccompanied as he doesn't want to get his feet soaked. Above the house the gum trees lean out over two dams. Up here the rich soil of the paddocks gives way to stony ground, and a patchwork of wildflowers grows between the grey, lichen-coated boulders.

Three months later we receive another call from the agent. 'The owners have gone broke, are you still interested in the house?'

Yes, definitely.

bulbine lily

I walk into the back garden the first morning after we have moved in and confront a scene straight from the classic Hitchcock horror movie, *The Birds*. Along the top of the fence a row of strange, black birds with hooked beaks stare down at me through glowing red

4

eyes. They don't attempt to fly away when I move towards them. Instead they begin to rock back and forth in unison, all the time letting out weird, breathy whistles. When they finally fly off I see they have white wing feathers.

Beside the house there's a large shed with an earth floor where the previous owners conducted their business of making concrete garden ornaments. A giraffe with a broken neck sits near the side gate and on the back verandah there's a whole farmyard of concrete chickens, ducks and small animals. My mother, who lives in a nearby retirement village, suggests the elderly people there might like them. Soon the animals have all found new homes and one old man, who's been a farmer all his life, is absolutely delighted to have chickens and ducks in his backyard again.

At night a dozen large spiders with red-striped legs construct huge webs across the verandah. They catch a multitude of tiny moths, attracted by the kitchen light. These same moths provide a welcome dinner for two small frogs lying in wait on the window.

The front of the property is divided by a broad irrigation channel, used to flood the paddocks in the days when they were part of a dairy farm. Contemplating the grassy, treeless area farthest from the house, we discuss its possible uses. In this, our first year at Clay Gully, our dams fill with water in the spring and thunderstorms replenish them in the summer. Good rains are predicted for next year offering us the opportunity to establish an agricultural enterprise. I think of goats and chickens but my husband, Nick, vetoes all my suggestions. He knows only too well that I can't kill anything and is already anticipating the vet bills involved in keeping alive aging hens, well past their egg-laying days.

A lover of good wine, his thoughts turn naturally to planting a vineyard, but I can see problems with this suggestion. Not having the necessary knowledge or equipment to process the grapes ourselves, we would be dependent on large wineries to take our fruit and set the price. Instead I think of the beautiful apples my grandfather grew in England – Bramley's Seedling, Lord Lambourne and Red Astrachan. There must be a market for these delicious, forgotten varieties. My grandfather grew them without artificial fertilisers or pesticides. We decide to follow the long path leading to full organic certification of the orchard.

It's necessary to have a third dam dug in front of the house and to purchase additional rural water. The contractor isn't pleased with me when I insist on having an island in the middle of the dam. It makes his job more difficult but I know it'll look beautiful and will be a refuge for water birds.

Then we discover Badgers Keep, a wonderful heritage apple nursery with over 500 different cultivars. With so many to choose from, I spend many hours poring over their descriptions. One apple we should definitely grow is the Bramley's Seedling. The population of the UK eats millions of Bramleys every year and I'm convinced that once Australians try them they will love them too. The variety has stood the test of time. The original tree, growing in a garden in Nottinghamshire, is still bearing fruit after 200 years.

Next I select Autumn Pearmain, striped and perfumed, and grown since the late 1500s. Then there is the Orleans Reinette, yellow, sweet and nutty, and the soft and juicy Beauty of Bath. My husband Nick, being Dutch, has his own favourite apple much loved on the continent. This is the Belle de Boskoop, sometimes known as Goudreinet. It has a strong flavour making it excellent for cooking. If left longer on the tree it turns into a fragrant, soft-pink dessert apple. We order the Bramley's Seedling and Belle de Boskoop and by the time we've selected enough cultivars for their pollination, we have twenty-four different varieties. In all there will be 300 trees.

For every tree there needs to be another which flowers at the same time, since apples are not normally self-fertile. There's a particular problem with both the Bramleys and Belle de Boskoop. They are triploid varieties, meaning their pollen is too weak to fertilise other trees. Therefore we must plant two pollinators together so they can impregnate each other as well as the Bramleys and Belles.

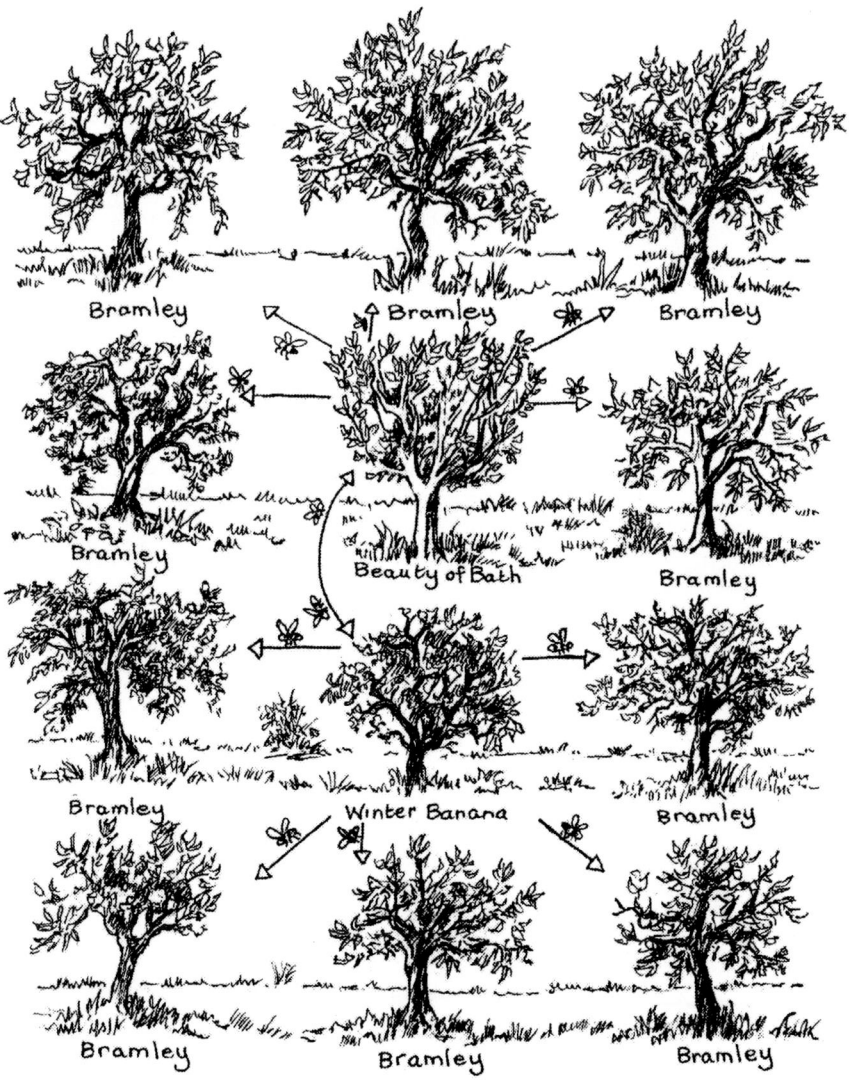

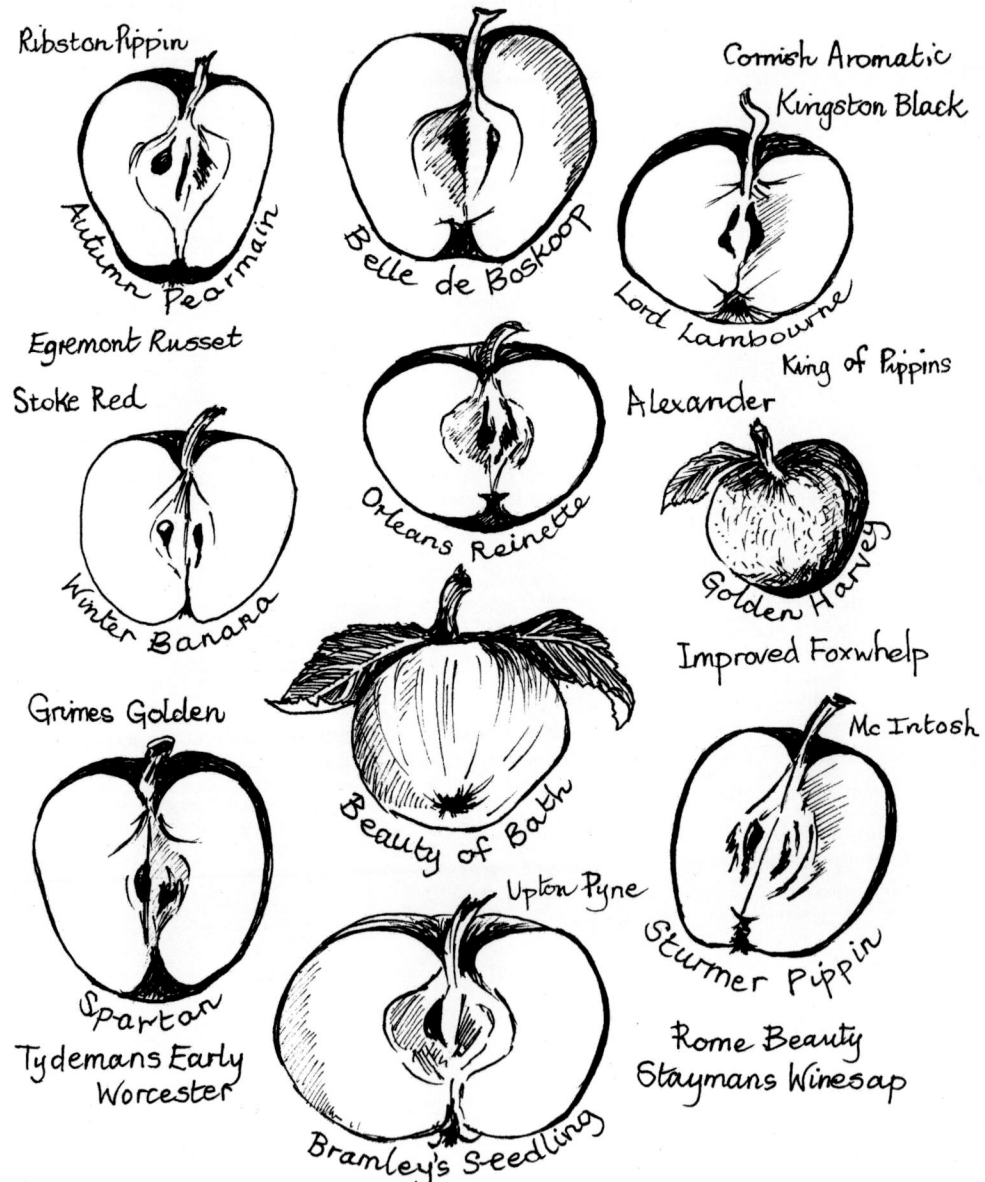

Nick, who was a marine engineer, prepares an amazing array of pumps and pipes. They can move the water from the three dams to wherever it's needed on the block. He draws me a diagram that I follow when I'm watering, but the system is so complex I feel as if I need marine training too.

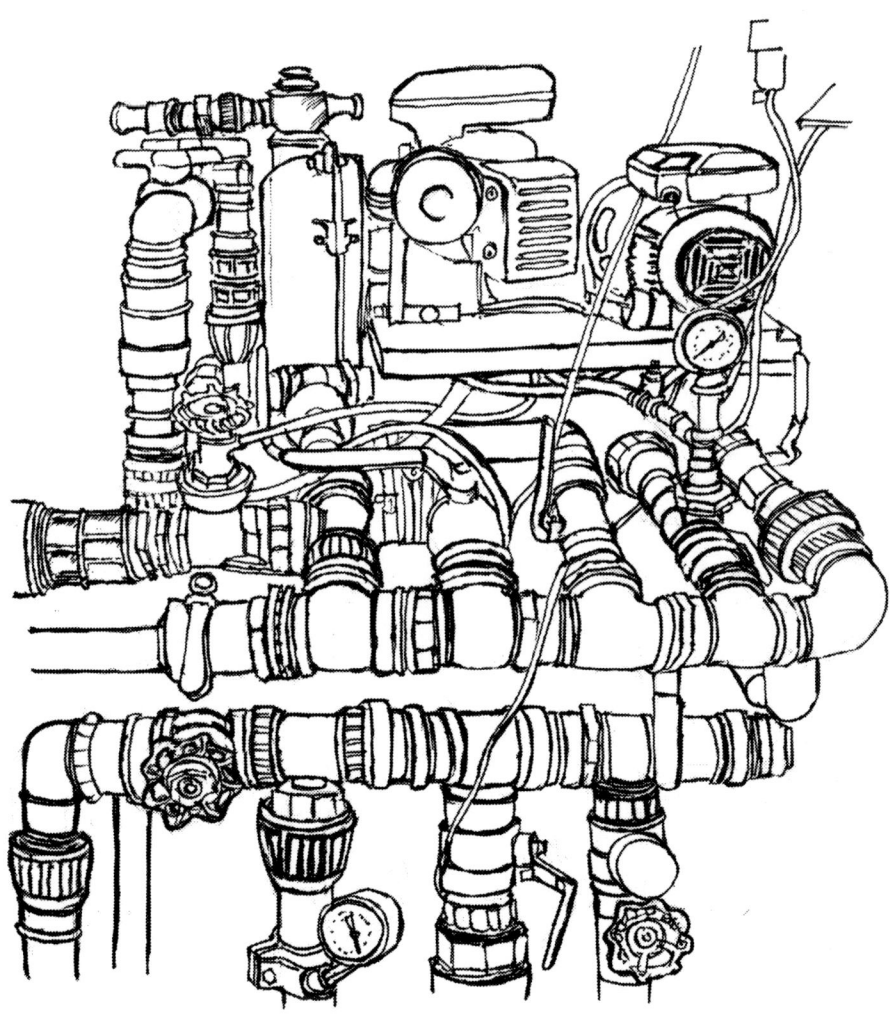

As my husband's other business becomes increasingly demanding, I find myself left with full responsibility for the orchard. Rightly described by Nick as a technical moron, I need to learn how to drive a tractor, cope with the irrigation system and become efficient with spray equipment. Fortunately he comes to my rescue when everything goes wrong, machinery breaks down or the pipes belch out water.

We decide to plant the orchard in stages, putting in 100 trees each year. This will allow enough time for us to prepare the land and for Clive and Margaret at Badgers Keep to graft the trees.

Behind the house the hillside is rocky with only a thin layer of soil; the pearly quartz is near the surface here. Although there's never been mining on our property, this white rock carries gold and the signs of digging and sluicing can be seen all through the surrounding bush. In some places in the forest there are hidden shafts, long since abandoned. It's best to keep to one of the many tracks left by the goldminers when you walk there.

Over the years rainwater has carried the soil from the hill and deposited it in the paddocks below the house, and here it's rich and deep. Our main concern at planting time is to ensure the trees don't get wet feet when rainwater floods down the hillside in the winter. For that reason we decide to plant them on raised beds.

The extra water needed for the trees is to be delivered through a water race. It runs for many kilometres through the

bush, servicing farms and villages along the way. After the bailiff opens the gate in the race, the water takes a whole day to run down the hill into our dam. Along the way it dislodges fallen leaves and branches. For the first two days we need to be ready with a spade to remove any blockages before the water overflows into the adjoining paddocks.

The spring rains continue and I decide to take advantage of them. Along the side of the orchard I dig in a row of native plants: bottlebrushes with fluffy red flowers, pale yellow melaleucas and purple kunzeas. In between I add a few small ornamental gum trees with curly grey, overlapping leaves. Hopefully these plants will encourage useful predatory insects to settle in the orchard and protect the apple trees.

Between the rows of apples I scatter subterranean clover seed which soon forms a thick green carpet. Although it dies back in the summer heat, it reappears when the rains return in the autumn. The nectar-rich flowers attract the bees and the roots improve the soil.

We plant a mixed orchard in front of the house. There are apricots, pears, greengage plums and a loquat tree. When the pistachios split open I bake them in the oven on beds of salt. After a while there are big bowls of red cherries to put on the table at Christmas.

I buy two olive trees from a Greek farmer at the market. He gives me a funny look when in my ignorance I ask him for black olive trees, not realising that olives change colour as they ripen. Italian friends show me how to cure the green ones, and some I leave to swell and turn shiny black. We serve them with drinks, sliced on pizzas and in a tuna tart. At the end of summer I pick the quinces and make a deep amber quince paste.

Quince Paste

When I make this the whole house fills with the delicate smell of the fruit. I don't recommend cooking too many quinces at a time because of the amount of stirring involved.

quinces
white sugar

Wash the quinces and wipe off the fur. Place them on a baking sheet. Roast in a slow oven until soft. Allow to cool. Then take out the cores and carefully remove any remaining seeds or stalk, but leave the skin on. Use a blender to turn the flesh into a smooth paste. Weigh it and measure out half that amount in white sugar. Combine the sugar and quince and stir well.

Put the mixture into a heavy bottomed pan and cook over a low heat. Stir frequently, especially towards the end of cooking to prevent burning. Depending on the quantity, this may take 2 hours or more.

When the mixture is very thick and pulls away from the sides and bottom of the pan, remove from the heat. Spread the mixture onto a baking tray lined with nonstick paper.

Slice and serve with cheese or dust with icing sugar and serve as a sweet.

Orange Pistachio Biscuits

These are thin, crisp biscuits with a delicate balance between the orange, pistachio and cardamom flavours.

160 grams unsalted pistachios
¾ cup caster sugar
1 egg, lightly beaten
1 heaped tablespoon self-raising flour
3 heaped teaspoons grated orange rind
1 level teaspoon ground cardamom

Pre-heat the oven to 160°C (or 150°C if fan forced). Line a baking tray with non-stick paper.

Halve or roughly chop 30 grams of the pistachios. Coarsely grind the remaining 130 grams in a food processor. Add the flour, sugar and other ingredients and stir well.

Place teaspoons of the mixture onto the tray 4 centimetres apart. Stud with the pistachio pieces and bake for approximately 10 minutes or until edges brown. Allow to cool before lifting onto a wire rack.

Olive and Tuna Tart

The strong taste of the olives and anchovies nicely contrasts with the blander tuna filling.

23 centimetre shortcrust pastry case
40 grams cornflour
400 millilitres milk
knob of butter
425 g can tuna in brine or spring water
¼ cup finely chopped parsley
1 tablespoon lemon juice
salt and pepper
45 grams anchovy fillets
1 ripe tomato
80 grams pitted olives (home grown, or for a decorative effect, red pimento stuffed)
lemon slice

Preheat the oven to 180°C. Prick the base of the flan case with a fork and bake blind for approximately 15 minutes. (Either cover the base with paper and baking beans or with pieces of crumpled foil.) Remove the foil/beans 5 minutes before the end of cooking. When lightly browned remove the case from the oven and allow to cool.

Dissolve the cornflour in 100 millilitres of the milk. Gently heat the remainder of the milk with a knob of butter. When almost boiling remove the pan from the heat and add the cornflour mixture stirring rapidly. Return to the stove and cook over a low heat continuing to stir until the sauce is smooth and thick. Remove from the heat.

Drain the tuna and place it in a bowl with the chopped parsley, lemon juice and salt and pepper. Stir in the white sauce.

When cool turn the mixture into the flan case. Lay the anchovies on top like the spokes of a wheel. Halve the tomato and place a thin slice between each anchovy. Cut the olives in half and place cut side up all around the edge of the tart and wherever else there is a space. Arrange a slice of lemon in the centre.

This is better if allowed to go cold and set in the fridge. Reheat next day in the oven or serve cold if preferred.

My elder son finds a chihuahua, which he names Stijl, wandering amongst the traffic on Lygon Street in Melbourne. He is the tiniest dog I have ever seen. It appears he has some sort of problem, for the tip of his tongue peeps permanently from the corner of his mouth. After a while Angus, who is still a student, is unable to keep him and so Stijl comes to live with us.

When friends visit they start to say, 'What a dear little . . .' but trail off when they see what is hanging underneath, for his penis is so long that it skims the floor. This may not have mattered when he lived in the city, but here the dust and dirt in the bush make him constantly sore. The vet tries medication and castration but to no avail. Finally we face the inevitable. At least half of it must be cut off. I am filled with guilt at putting him through such a dreadful operation, but within a couple of days he is fine and running through the bush with the other dogs.

I don't know how old he is but he has few teeth and there is white hair around his muzzle. When, after a few years, he dies suddenly from a heart attack I am devastated. My husband, concerned, goes to Melbourne and returns with a chihuahua pup. This one is jet black. I ask Nick what the parents were like, but

Reuben

he hasn't seen them. After a few weeks the puppy grows a small grey beard and I know something is wrong. Shortly afterwards the spindly legs suddenly sprout and he looks like a chihuahua on stilts. When I open the door he circles the paddock, running so fast I can only make out a black blur. This is no chihuahua. Still, we come to love this sweet, quiet dog. We call him Reuben. He is my shadow.

Although I love Reuben dearly, I still miss Stijl and long for another chihuahua. After some persuasion Nick gives in and we adopt a third dog, a companion for Reuben and our German shorthaired pointer, Coby.

He is a little grey-coated fellow with white bib and paws. We check his parents to make sure this one is indeed a chihuahua. Typical of his breed, José is all front and false courage. Despite his size he soon has our other dogs under control. He makes himself useful by immediately assuming the role of guard dog, and warning us of approaching strangers.

Soon after moving in, I discover a narrow path leading up the hill beyond our house to a large dam hidden in the bush. It's quite beautiful, and is an ideal place for the dogs to have a walk or swim. I take them up there every morning before I go to work and, as usual, our shorthaired pointer vanishes into the bush in search of rabbits. I let her go, since she always reappears just as I return to our gate. For company I have my chihuahua, José, but today he's slow and lags behind. When I realise he isn't following me I turn back in time to see a magpie watching him closely from a bough of yellow wattle. Suddenly the bird flies down and struts purposefully towards the dog, now standing frozen on the path. I have visions of what a big sharp beak could do to a tiny chihuahua, and quickly scoop him out of harm's way before continuing my walk.

With a sudden rustle of feathers the magpie alights on my shoulder. He's clearly mesmerised by this creature, too small to be a dog but without the necessary ears to be a rabbit. I continue to follow the path through the trees with a dog on one arm and the bird on the other, staring into each other's eyes in fascination. Just as we reach the gate the magpie flies off.

Now I call out whenever I see a magpie and sometimes it turns out to be 'my' bird. He follows me, fluttering from tree to tree along the side of the path. When I reach the big dam he flies down to sit on my shoulder, where he stays until I finish my circuit of the bush. Just as I reach the gate at the end of my walk he flies away, perhaps because our property is another bird's territory.

There are twenty-four different apple tree cultivars that need to be labelled in a way that can be easily seen. At first I buy plastic tags and push them into the ground next to the trunks, but they're soon displaced by large kangaroo feet. Then I try hanging the tags in the trees, but once summer comes they're too difficult to find amongst the foliage. Finally, after looking around the recycling shop at the local tip, I return home with two old venetian blinds. When cut into good-sized lengths and written on in pencil, they make perfect labels.

One morning there's a hare in the orchard. I always assumed hares were just like large rabbits, but this is a far more impressive animal. For a moment I mistake it for a dog. This is partly because of its size but also because of the way it runs rather than hops. It stops just long enough for me to see that its enormous ears are tipped with black. I know hares will strip the bark from the young trees, so now something must be done to protect them.

I see that the professional apple growers in the Harcourt Valley use insulation paper, blue on one side and silver on the other. I buy a large roll and spend the next two mornings taping pieces of it around the trunks of the trees. For a few weeks that seems to solve the problem. Then I spot a magpie attacking one of the new guards, apparently attracted to its shiny surface. Within a few days most of the paper rolls are in tatters and little pieces of foil are blowing all over the orchard. Maybe they don't have magpies in Harcourt.

After removing the damaged guards I fasten them back on to the trees with the intact blue paper on the outside. For a while that seems to work. Then one night there's a big storm with driving rain, and the next day the paper is a soggy mess. Nick suggests I use plastic gutter guard and fasten it to the trees with a long stapler. Obviously this material is waterproof and it shouldn't attract the magpies either.

It isn't until early summer that I begin to notice guards lying on the earth beside the trees. More fall off every day and it seems I can't have fastened them on firmly enough. I staple them back in place and then work my way through the entire orchard, reinforcing the remainder. Within days they are all lying on the ground again.

Walking through the orchard, I notice that just ahead of me two powerfully built crow-like birds are strutting between the trees. They're grey currawongs. As I watch, one of the birds suddenly pushes its heavy beak inside a tree guard and forcefully rips the staples loose. When the plastic drops to the ground the other bird hurries across to join its partner, and together they fall upon the spiders and beetles which have made the dark interior of the guard their home. Now I know what's happening, so this time I tie the strips back onto the trees with hay-bale twine. And there they remain.

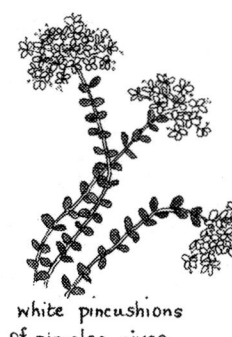
white pincushions of pimelea nivea

In late winter we add another six rows to the orchard. The final 100 trees will go in next year. After considering our water situation we decide to plant a variety of Australian natives suitable for cut flowers. We have been told there is likely to be a strong market for them, and they could provide additional income.

Between the apple trees we grow dainty pink wax flowers interspersed with pimelea. That has dark leaves on interesting, hairy white stalks, making it useful in flower arrangements. At Christmas the persoonias produce long heads of yellow flowers on spruce-like foliage. The tea-tree bushes at the bottom of the orchard are spectacular in springtime when they are covered with a mass of lavender flowers.

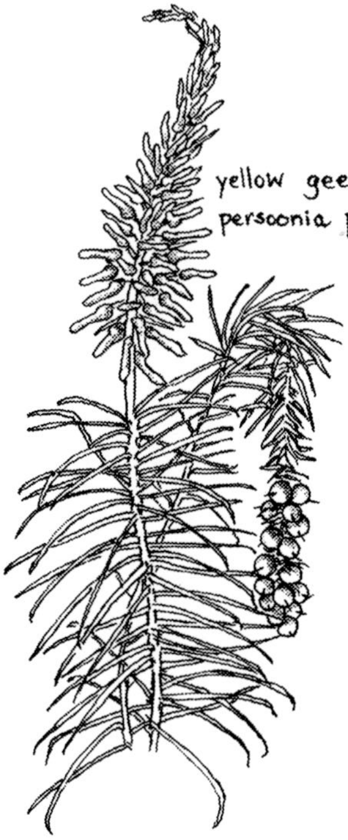

yellow geebung persoonia pinifolia

lavender tea tree

pale pink NSW wax flower

In the front garden rosellas feed on the native hibiscus. Crested pigeons and wattlebirds drink from the fountain and a Pacific black duck dabbles at its base.

In the early spring the front paddock becomes a nursery as young joeys take their first steps outside the pouch. Soon they race round in circles on gawky legs, before returning to their mothers for another feed.

Until now, when I thought of a baby kangaroo, I always envisaged a sweet little face peeping out of a pouch. I didn't realise how much joeys wriggle around inside. It can't be easy for their mothers to suddenly have to manage an extra tail or pair of legs.

I am thrilled to have large wild animals in my backyard.

When I was growing up in England, there were only the blue tits and robins which drank from the old church font my mother used as a birdbath. Seeing brilliantly coloured parrots in the garden, I still feel as if I'm at the zoo.

In a gust of wind five brown-headed honeyeaters flutter down like falling leaves into the tecoma bush beside the bedroom window. They've come for the nectar hidden inside its showy orange trumpets. Every morning I hear the piping call of the eastern spinebill, so loud and piercing for such a small bird. He swoops down to the low-growing correa bushes, where he dips his fine curved beak into their pink and cream bells. Then he, too, visits the tecoma flowers, but in a few brief moments he's gone and won't return until the same time tomorrow.

Every few days I find an eggshell in the grass. I know our neighbour keeps chickens and I'm concerned.

Reuben regularly patrols our boundary. He may have somehow found his way into the henhouse and helped himself to a few treasures. At other times there's a golf ball lying in the orchard or on the driveway. Apparently one of our neighbours has been practising his strokes, indifferent to where the ball might land. I feel rather indignant. We shall have broken windows next.

One bright morning I take José, my chihuahua, for a walk. As usual he's doing his bizarre steeplechasing thing, galloping crosswise through the orchard and leaping over each mounded row in turn. Just ahead of us a currawong is busily working at some item of food with his powerful beak. Resenting the intrusion, he hops a little distance away as I look to see what he's been eating. There in the grass is half a golf ball. I suddenly realise I have discovered both a golf ball and an egg thief. Currawongs are wily birds but they obviously aren't able to differentiate between a ball and a hen's egg.

We live in Box Ironbark Forest. The bark of the box trees is pale and flaky, but the tough ironbarks have deep fissures and are so dark you could think they had been through a bushfire. At the highest corner of the orchard stands a huge gum tree, a yellow box. It's very different from the surrounding red and grey boxes. The leaves of this towering tree are small and held in delicate cloudy fronds against the sky. Deep in a cleft in its trunk lives a swarm of wild bees.

All around the house, birds are nesting. Right by the back door a pair of silvereyes builds a home in the climbing grape ivy. Soon there are three blue-green eggs in the nest. The birds are indifferent to our presence and even barking dogs don't seem to bother them.

The fairy wrens make their nest in the dense centre of the banksia rose by the side gate. Not long after they raise their first family they begin the whole process again, this time among the blue flowers of the plumbago bush at the back of the house. Early one morning three tiny babies fly the nest but don't know how to escape from the shadecloth-covered verandah. The adult birds call plaintively to them from their perch on a wattle bush in the back garden, but to no avail. Finally I cup my hands around each fluttering baby and carry it up the steps to its waiting parents.

Just behind the house the white winged choughs work together to build their nest. The birds carry mud from the top dam to a red box tree, where they form a smooth clay bowl in the fork of two horizontal branches. Although only one bird lays the eggs, they all take it in turns to sit on the nest and feed the young when they hatch. The family continues to use this sturdy bowl for several seasons before it eventually crumbles away. The swallows use mud too, to make their nest under the wooden eaves of the front verandah. They swoop over the orchard catching tiny flies on the wing, and return to feed their nestlings every two or three minutes.

The spotted pardalotes, tiny and brilliantly coloured, make their nest each year in a tunnel they have dug between the sleepers on the verandah. Completely unafraid, the birds perch on the vine just above our heads while we are eating dinner. They dive down behind our chairs to deliver butterflies and moths to their babies hidden below the garden bed.

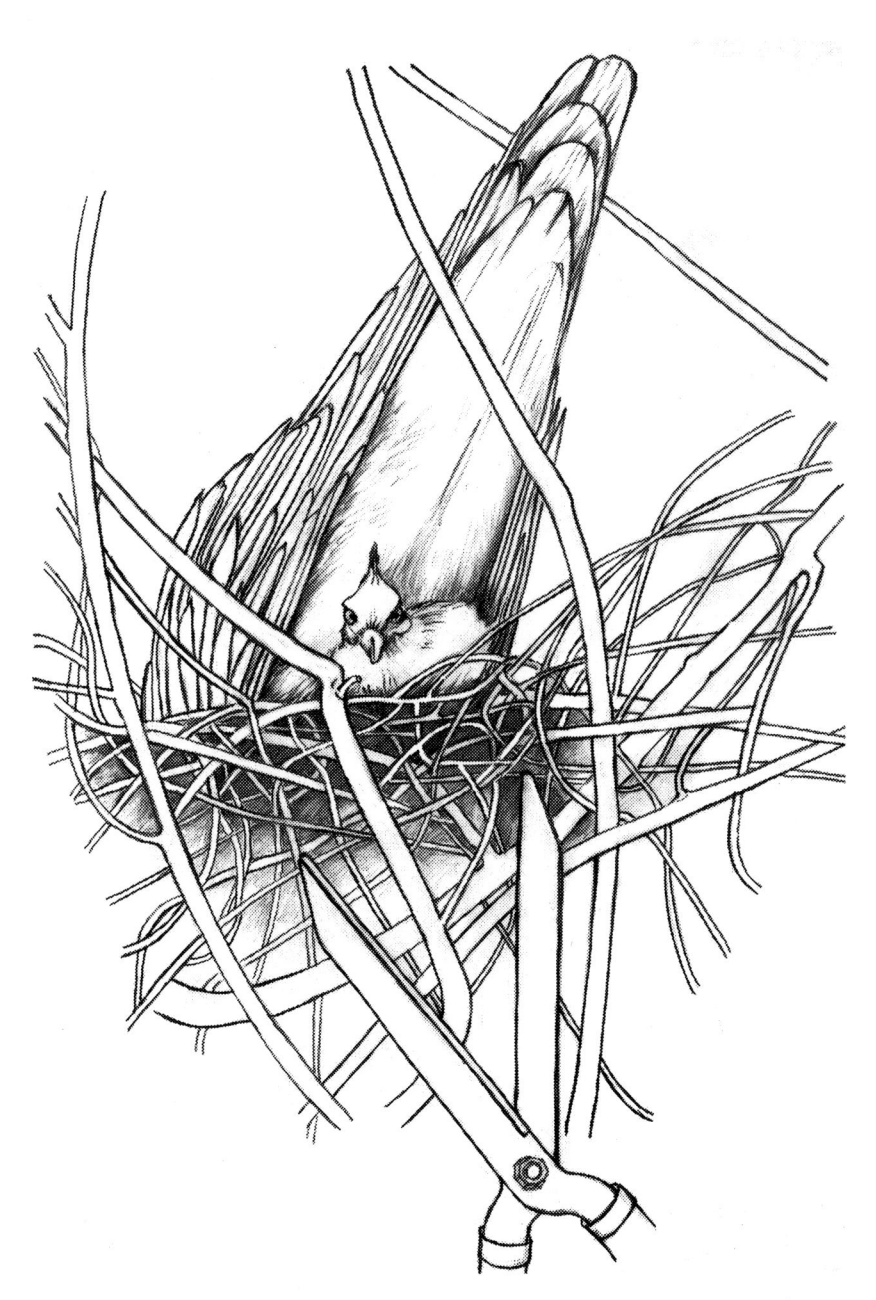

Les, my friend and helper, prunes the plants in the front garden. When he begins work on the purple buddleia bush he narrowly avoids cutting off a pigeon's tail.

It's been raining heavily and the grass is lush and long. Since what I think of as my 'Great Snake Experience' I am deathly afraid of stepping into long grass. One afternoon I had taken my elderly mother to the sewage works. That may seem strange, but she's a nature lover and all kinds of interesting birds congregate there. We walked along a narrow path which gradually became more and more overgrown and I knew it was time to turn around.

At that moment I felt something move against my leg at the front of my thigh. I glanced down and was horrified to see the body of a large brown snake protruding from the hem of my jeans. By instinct I flicked my leg forward, forcibly ejecting the thick coils into the air. The snake made its escape and disappeared into the undergrowth.

I could hardly believe what I had seen, but when I turned to my mother in amazement, I saw her face had turned a pasty white and I knew it had really happened. Two thoughts came to me. Firstly, that it's dangerous to move after being bitten as that hastens the spread of the venom. Second, that nobody knew we were there and my mother wouldn't be able to go for help alone. Although I felt no pain, I wasn't sure whether it was possible to be bitten by a snake without feeling it. I ripped down my jeans, searching for a bite mark. There was none. Trembling, I took my mother's arm and carefully avoiding the patches of long grass, we stumbled back to the car.

Afterwards I wondered why I had been spared. Perhaps it was nature's way of repaying me for all the small animals, beetles and spiders I'd rescued over the years. Later I thought of the more prosaic possibility that the snake would have needed to draw back its head before striking and there wasn't enough space for that inside my jeans.

Keen to keep the grass short in the orchard, I spend three happy days sitting on the mower enjoying the sweet smell of hay drying in the sun. This is easy work. I delight in the appearance of the neat green avenues being created, as perfect as any retiree's lovingly attended patch of lawn.
I can't mow close to the trees because of the low hanging branches and the wildflowers growing along the rows. Here the grass is long and is interspersed by tough reeds and the occasional Scotch thistle.

Once the mowing is completed I spend the next few days down on my knees pulling out great piles of weeds. After a while I realise that if I don't get some assistance, by the time I reach the last row the grass will have regrown in the first. There's a man who does garden work who agrees to come and help me. Now I have someone to chat to while I'm weeding, and within a day or so we reach the final rows. Deep in thought, I am tugging at an especially tough reed when I hear a sudden cry. My fellow worker runs towards me, his face ashen. After he regains his breath, he tells me that he pulled out a dense clump of grass only to find a very surprised brown snake in it's midst. Fortunately neither man nor snake came to any harm.

33

I've bought a book of Scott Joplin rags. They are difficult to play but I'm determined to master them. It's a beautiful spring morning and I should be outside thinning the fruit right now, but first I sit down at the piano for another attempt at playing 'The Entertainer'. Our aging shorthaired pointer, Coby, likes to follow me into the orchard. She lies under the shade of a nearby tree and watches me while I'm working.

Now she sighs once before coming to sit beside the piano. She's patient for a while, but when I turn the pages and begin to play another favourite, 'The Rose Leaf Rag', she lets out a small plaintive cry, for she wants to be outside. Lost in the music, I don't notice when she lies down and shuffles under the piano. That is, until I next try to use the pedal. There is the firm pressure of a paw on top of my foot and I know it's time to go to work.

Her mouth is highly sensitive. We often eat fried rice with chopped vegetables, and Coby enjoys the leftovers. The only problem is that they contain peas and she hates them. After taking each mouthful she sorts through the rice and drops a few, perfectly cleaned, back into her bowl. In the autumn, when I walk with her up to the far dam, she stops briefly at a small blackberry bush growing there to eat the fruit. It's covered with ferocious thorns but she delicately nips off each berry without being pricked.

Spring moves into summer and at the end of a very hot day I need to run the irrigation for a while. Some time later when I go to check, I notice one of the drippers has blown off and water is arcing through the air. Immediately beneath it a grey crested pigeon is lying motionless on its side. One wing is pointing upwards, only moving slightly when it's caught by the wind. I hurry off to find a replacement dripper, wondering what has killed the bird and why a fox hasn't taken it away. Upon my return I'm amazed to see that the 'dead' pigeon has now been joined by two others. They are all lying closely together in a row. Each one has a wing outstretched, carefully directing the cool water into its 'armpit'.

The water has run for long enough and now that it's almost dark I go down to turn off the irrigation. In the twilight I can dimly make out the shape of a kangaroo in the lower orchard. At the head of each row of pipes I stop to turn off the handle to the valve. I do this efficiently – walk, bend, turn, walk, bend, turn – engrossed in the familiar task. Three rows from the bottom I bend, turn, straighten up, and there in the next row a huge male kangaroo is standing directly in my path. I stop dead and we look into each other's eyes. We are both in shock.

His face is beautiful, kindly, but now I look at the enormous black claws held close to his chest, and I'm afraid. I lower my eyes and turn my face from him. One frozen moment later, he slowly turns and quietly lopes away.

A line is drawn across the upper paddock and although it's invisible, I know exactly where it runs. Above it the white-winged choughs are free to move as they will in their search for food, but below it is magpie territory. Once the choughs cross over the border they're in danger of attack.

For a while the birds spread out and run around like chickens, digging into the soil in their search for bugs or seed. When a bird finds something good to eat, it runs to one of the two waiting fledglings and pops it into its beak. The whole family shares in the care of these youngsters.

Then they're spotted by a magpie that swoops down on them aggressively. The choughs, however, don't seem particularly concerned and the attacker soon flies away. A few minutes later it returns with its partner and together they harass the little clan by repeated dive bombing.

It seems one magpie is manageable but two magpies are not. Whistling loudly, the birds cluster tightly together in a circle with wings outspread and tails bobbing. The magpies land on the ground beside them. Single file, the red-eyed gang is frog-marched back up the hill with the magpies close at its heels. Once the birds cross over the invisible line the magpies immediately turn back, leaving the choughs in peace, until next time.

Over summer our young saplings double in size. Then comes autumn and high winds blow away the browning leaves. In another month the trees are dormant. It's time to prune and to dig in fertiliser for next season.

Towards the end of winter, Nick fastens a wooden nesting box to a tree at the edge of the orchard. We're hoping the eastern rosellas will find it. They're such stunning birds with their red, yellow, green and blue plumage. I check the box regularly but when spring comes, no birds have taken up residence.

Then as I walk past the big tree early one morning, I have a feeling of being watched. Glancing up, I see a tiny striped head and two bright eyes peering out at me. It's a sugar glider. For a few moments he studies me seriously, and then he returns to his sleep in the dark depths of the box. That evening I return just as the last light is fading, and I'm rewarded by the sight of three of the tiny, fairylike, creatures. They're having a wonderful time chasing each other up and down the trunk of the big yellow box tree.

PART TWO

Bramleys, Bees and Button Quail

One evening, just after the apple blossom has begun to open, Michael the beekeeper arrives with three hives. He comes at dusk, having waited for the bees to return home from their daytime foraging, and places the hives at the top of the orchard near the yellow box tree.

Some time later he returns in daylight. On his head he wears a veil and he gives each hive a puff of smoke to calm the bees. I stand at a safe distance, watching with interest. Michael lifts out the frames carrying the honeycomb, searches for the queens and checks to see how much honey has been made. He wears a long-sleeved shirt, but soon several bees disappear inside his cuff and proceed to walk up his arm. Periodically he gives a little cry and swats at his sleeve, remarking that the stings are always more painful early in the season.

As a child I was stung several times by my grandfather's bees and know how agonising that can be, so I watch Michael with growing admiration. Suddenly a bee is caught in my hair, and before I can set it free it stings me on the back of my head. Michael looks up when I cry out in pain and briefly remarks, 'One got you did it?' before returning to his work.

I stand stoically in the same spot, and it isn't until he puts the lids back on the hives and drives away that I make a frantic dash for the house, by now desperate to find something to relieve the pain.

A few days later my son Nathaniel comes to see the orchard in all its glory. The dainty apple blossom is fully out, and so are the pink wax flowers and pretty white pincushion heads of the pimeleas. We can hear the steady drone of the bees as they move from flower to flower collecting yellow bags of pollen, and at the same time fertilising the blossom. As we wander through the orchard I stop for a moment, telling Nat how I was standing in just this spot when I was stung the previous week. Immediately he gives a cry of pain and slaps at his ear, where he too has suddenly been stung.

I'm regularly surrounded by bees when I'm working in the orchard but have never been attacked until now, so this seems strange. We aren't close to the hives but perhaps we are intruders crossing a vital, but unseen, flight path.

It's been ten days since Michael brought the bees. I can tell they've done their work for the powdery yellow pollen has gone from the stamens of the blossom. In addition to Michael's brown striped honeybees, tiny native bees hover around the flowers, and here and there a large black bee dips its head into a bloom.

Then the steady background drone changes to a higher pitched, more urgent sound, and soon an angry swarm circles above the trees. As the noise grows louder I know it's time to leave and I break into a run. Two bees chase after me, buzzing angrily around my head but I manage to escape them.

In the afternoon when the swarm settles on a low branching tree, I telephone Michael to let him know. He comes with an empty hive which he places directly beneath the bees. With one sharp tap of the branch the swarm drops neatly into the box as if it were a single organism, rather than a group of hundreds of individuals. Michael quickly replaces the lid and leaves the bees to adapt to their new home.

Between the house and the bottom dam there stands a beautiful red flowering ironbark, its blossoms hanging down in sweet smelling sprays. Bees fly to and fro between this tree and the remaining apple blossom. The raucous cries of wattlebirds and blue-faced honeyeaters can be heard all day long as they feed greedily on the rich nectar.

Michael gives me a bucket of honey. It is thick and rich amber. It comes from the flowers of the graceful yellow gum trees. We eat it on toast and I add its delicate flavour to my cakes.

Cold Tea Cake

Sixty years ago this was one of my mother's favourite recipes, probably because it is so easy and quick to make. In our house it was served together with a piece of cheddar cheese and a slice of apple.

⅓ cup honey
⅓ cup brown sugar
1 cup strong tea
250 grams currants
100 grams raisins
225 grams self-raising flour
1 egg, beaten

Dissolve the honey and sugar in the hot tea, pour onto the fruit and leave overnight. Next day add the flour and beaten egg and stir well.

Put into a greased and lined loaf tin and bake at 160°C (or 150°C if fan forced), for approximately 70 minutes. Test with a skewer near to time and continue cooking until it comes out clean.

Dutch Honey Cake

This is a traditional Dutch recipe dating back centuries. It is usually served buttered and eaten with coffee. The ginger pieces are optional, but they add flavour and texture.

250 grams self-raising flour
2 teaspoons ground cinnamon
1½ teaspoons ground ginger
½ teaspoon ground cloves
½ teaspoon ground nutmeg
150 grams chopped glace ginger
150 grams brown sugar
½ cup + 1 dessertspoon of honey
¾ cup milk

Sift the flour and spices into a bowl. Mix in the chopped ginger making sure the pieces are well coated with flour. Add the sugar, honey and milk and stir well.

Pour into a greased, lined loaf tin and cook at 160°C (or 150°C if fan forced) for approximately one hour. Towards the end of cooking check with a skewer and when it comes out clean remove the cake from the oven. Leave for a few minutes and then turn out onto a wire tray.

There's a black plastic box fixed to a post on the verandah. It houses the transformer for the garden watering system. Whenever children come to visit, I invite them to look inside to see the frog that lives in its dark interior. He's been in the box for the last two years, apparently having entered through the small hole drilled into the base. His brown mottled body is quite fat, and it's difficult to imagine how he could squeeze through such a little space.

Perhaps he has eaten too many flies or spiders inside the box and can no longer get out. I leave the door ajar for a while but he remains in his place, squatting on top of the transformer. Mostly, we forget he's there. After a shower of rain, however, his piercing *crack-crack* echoes around the house and reminds us of his existence.

On the first day since winter warm enough to sit outside, I carry my cup of tea onto the verandah. A small movement catches my eye and startled, I see a slim brown snake emerging from the transformer box. I usher the dogs quickly into the house, feeling sad that our frog has clearly met his end. Then I watch the snake swing to and fro, expecting it to slide out and disappear. No more of the snake's body emerges, apparently because its frog-filled lower section is now too fat to squeeze through the hole in the box. All day long the little snake writhes in the air, suspended, and it is not until late the following afternoon that the frog is sufficiently digested for it to escape.

Noisy miners have established a small colony in the gum trees near the road. They have grey bodies and bright yellow beaks. Honeyeaters and native to Australia, they are unlike the scavenging common mynas seen in urban settings. True to their name they make a lot of noise so I'm glad they rarely come close to the house. I only notice them when a fox or cat enters our property. Suddenly there's a huge commotion. The birds swoop down on the invading animal, squawking and shrieking to drive it away.

One afternoon I hear their cries and go to see why they are panicking. I'm concerned there might be a cat around because a family of wrens is nesting in a low bush near the dam. Instead I'm surprised to discover it's an echidna. He's huge. I haven't seen one on our block before. He's wandering along searching for ants, and takes no notice of either me or the screaming birds. In a few minutes he squeezes under the fence and disappears. I can understand the noisy miners' alarm at the appearance of feral animals, but I'm surprised a harmless echidna would frighten them. Perhaps they haven't seen one before either.

Two wood ducks stand close together on top of one of the nesting boxes. They look strange. I've never seen ducks in trees before. Quite beautiful with their chestnut heads and pale mottled breasts, they're more like finely built geese. The birds take it in turns to bend over and peer into the box. Then suddenly the female thrusts her plump brown body through the hole and disappears inside. I'm amazed there's enough space. She fails to reappear, but just as I begin to wonder if she's stuck, out she pops, and they both fly off.

My bird book tells me it's quite normal for wood ducks to nest in trees, but I'm left wondering how the flightless ducklings manage to leave the nest safely. Although I'm delighted to have them visit, I'm not sure about them breeding far away from the safety of the dam, especially since I've seen foxes recently.

I don't need to worry for by the time they return for the next house inspection, the galahs have already taken up residence and chase the ducks away. A few weeks later, as the orchard is bathed in golden evening sunlight, I see them again. This time they are accompanied by seven little ducklings, spreading out all around them as they wander along the rows of trees, grazing on the clover. Over the next few weeks I often see them just about sunset. Eventually they manage to raise five of their babies.

Now the white-faced heron has returned to take up his vigil beside the top dam. With limitless patience he waits motionless for small yabbies or tadpoles to unwarily swim close to his long dark legs. Occasionally, when the catch is unsatisfactory, he tries his luck in the bottom dam, flying above the trees with slow sweeping wing beats. At once a small flock of tiny but fearless birds flies up to harass him. They circle around him until he swoops down to the water again.

It's nine years since we planted the first rows of apple trees and, at last, more than half of the orchard has flowered.

I carry a small pair of nail scissors into the orchard and contemplate the 300 trees before me. Where there was blossom there's now fruit, with clusters of five or six apples standing close together on their little green stalks. Unless they're properly thinned I could have a huge crop the size of marbles.

In a non-organic orchard a chemical thinner would be applied to the blossom to reduce the fruit set, doing away with the need for hand thinning. I don't have this option. At least I can select the best fruit and choose its position on the branch. So every morning my scissors squeeze between the tight little clusters of apples as I slowly move around the trees. My legs begin to ache, the result of hours of standing, and I wonder if I could use a tall bar stool. Unfortunately four legs won't balance on the sloping mounds.

Never mind, this is light work. The birds are singing, the days are growing warmer and the bees are humming in the clover. What better place to work could there be than this? Two weeks later I have finished. And in no time the rosellas are trying the fledgling apples.

There are good rains in the spring, and twice in the early summer thunderstorms replenish the dams. The trees, appreciative of all the moisture around their roots, have grown strongly, and this year, for the first time, we have a marketable crop.

Every day I walk along the green avenues between the trees, admiring the swelling fruit. The Tydeman's Early Worcesters are beautiful, each tree filled with shiny red apples so perfect they would have tempted Snow White. There have been a few brightly coloured rosellas in the orchard recently, and here and there I can see where they have left a half eaten apple, its yellow centre exposed, as a welcome dinner for the ants.

A friend tells me parrots are afraid of snakes, so I buy two dozen rubber ones from a toy shop and hang them in the branches. I don't know if rosellas are not afraid of snakes or perhaps just too smart to be fooled by bits of rubber, but they're soon in the trees again eating the apples. This is a good crop and if the currawongs enjoy the windfalls or the parrots take an occasional apple, there is still enough for all. Nature must have her share.

It's a beautiful morning with just a light breeze gently disturbing the upper branches of the gum trees. I think that tomorrow we'll pick the Tydeman's, which are always the first to ripen. Although the other apples aren't ready yet, there's now a soft pink blush where their faces turn to the sun.

Suddenly I become aware of an unfamiliar sound. It's a murmuring, twittering buzz of excitement, growing stronger every moment. Now the air is filled with wings, swooping and diving above my head. Gradually the noise reduces as a hundred parrots land in the apple trees before making their way along the boughs towards the fruit.

They've come from nowhere. I've never seen them before and I am stunned by their beauty. There's a flash of red and blue, but they redefine the whole meaning of the word 'green'. This is a green like I have never seen; glorious, glossy, and unimaginably brilliant against the backdrop of emerald leaves and shiny red fruit. The birds, which have short blunt tails, don't have the gracious, swooping flight of the rosellas. These musk lorikeets are more like fighter planes on a mission.

A moment of joy and delight is swiftly followed by the realisation that these little beauties are attacking my apples. Rushing towards them, I wave my arms frantically, shouting, screaming and expecting the whole flock to rise up in panic. Nothing happens. As I hurl myself like a whirling dervish at a tree under attack, the parrots casually flutter into another one farther along the row. When I follow they just return to the original tree. They are treating me with derision. They just don't care. To think that at one point I considered putting a scarecrow in the orchard. Ridiculous! Not even a living, breathing, screaming human being is going to deter these birds.

The next day they are gone and all is peaceful. I expect the ripe Tydeman's to be ruined, so with some trepidation I walk along the rows surveying the damage. For a moment I feel a flood of relief, for the trees are still full of apples. It's only when I look closely that I realise a tiny piece of flesh has been removed from each one. Even those not yet fully ripe have been carefully assessed by an experienced avian eye. In each apple a little hole has been pecked in the very centre of that first small area of pink blush. There will be no crop this year after all. I collect the remaining apples which, though imperfect, are fine for sauces and chutneys.

Apple Chutney

Good to eat with cheese and biscuits, this chutney is fruity and spicy but not hot.

120 grams onions
4 cloves garlic
15 large cooking apples
500 grams brown sugar
1800 millilitres malt vinegar
2 teaspoons ground ginger
250 grams raisins
50 grams mustard seed
1 tablespoon salt
15 grams chilli powder

Mince the onions and garlic together. Peel, core and slice the apples. Boil the apples and sugar together in the vinegar until they are soft.

Add the other ingredients and simmer gently for 15 to 20 minutes. To prevent the mixture from burning, stir frequently with a wooden spoon. Allow to cool before bottling.

Red Cabbage with Apple

This is a lovely sweet and sour way to cook cabbage.

50 grams butter
1 cup water
½ teaspoon salt
600 grams red cabbage, chopped
2 cooking apples, peeled, cored and sliced
1 teaspoon ground cloves
1 tablespoon sugar
1 tablespoon white wine vinegar
pepper

Place 25 grams butter together with the water and salt in a saucepan. Add the red cabbage, apples and ground cloves. Bring to the boil and cover. Simmer for about 40 minutes or until the cabbage is soft, stirring occasionally. Add the sugar, vinegar, pepper and remaining butter. Simmer for another 5 minutes. Stir and serve.

Apple Sauce

This is good with Granny Smiths but brilliant with Bramley's Seedling.

4 green apples (preferably Bramleys) peeled, cored and chopped
50 grams butter
1 tablespoon water
a strip of lemon rind
approx. 50 grams caster sugar (depending on the variety of apple used)

Put the apples, butter, water, lemon rind and 20 grams sugar into a pan and cover. Place on a low heat stirring occasionally, for about 15 minutes or until the apples break down.

Remove from the heat. Break up any lumps with a fork. Add more sugar to taste and heat through again.

Early one morning there are rabbits running between the apple trees. As responsible landowners I know we should keep them under control, but I couldn't face killing a rabbit (nor even a spider for that matter). In any case their burrows aren't on our block. As soon as they are disturbed they race up the hill beyond the dam and disappear into the bush. They're the usual nondescript brown rabbits, but then one morning I spy a beautiful golden one – perhaps someone's escaped pet.

Over the next few months I see this rabbit more and more often, until it occurs to me that I'm probably also seeing his sons and daughters; possibly even his grandchildren. Now the small plants in the front garden are disappearing, and I can see that this influx is going to become a real problem. Then upon waking early one misty winter morning, I see a family of foxes just in front of the house. Two young cubs are chasing each other up and over my little stack of straw bales in the pale dawn light. And it isn't long before the rabbits are gone.

Last season the majority of the apples were ruined by the parrots, but those we managed to salvage tasted wonderful. Unfortunately some had the telltale hole indicating codling moth damage. This moth is responsible for the famous 'worm in the apple' and the well-known question: 'What is worse than a worm in your apple?'

Answer: 'Half a worm.'

Non-organic orchards are repeatedly sprayed with chemicals to control this pest. Instead, I hang traps in the trees which tell me if the moths are flying. When I catch a few, I order trichogramma wasps from Queensland. These tiny creatures use the moth eggs as a breeding site and in so doing, destroy them. The wasp eggs arrive in little squares of cardboard which I staple onto the apple leaves. I also buy 1200 ties to fasten onto the upper branches of the trees. These little pieces of plastic carry female moth pheromone which confuses the male moths, making it difficult for them to find their partner for mating.

I can hear a steady tapping coming from the shed. Our young Slovenian friend must be here again. He has recently arrived in Australia and speaks only a little English. He's extremely slim with pale skin and dark hair, and is easily the tallest person I have met. Good with his hands, he makes letter boxes, house signs, and small sculptures out of copper. He uses our shed for this purpose because at home his neighbours will not tolerate the noise. To return the favour he repeatedly offers to help me in the orchard, but I'm pruning and like to do that myself.

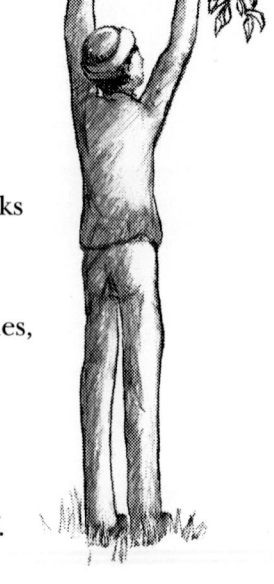

When I'm finished it's time to put on the pheromone ties. For every tree I have to move the ladder around and climb up and down four times to place them correctly. After completing the first row my legs are aching. Suddenly it occurs to me this would be an ideal job for my tall friend. Because of his height he doesn't need to use the ladder at all, so the job takes him a fraction of the time it would have taken me. We are both happy.

It's spring again, and a pair of pink and grey galahs has taken up residence in the nesting box nearest to the house. Although parrots don't make proper nests, the more richly coloured male brings token sprigs of gum leaf to his partner inside. They're a loving couple who sit on top of the box rubbing their beaks together and preening each other. I can tell the eggs have hatched when I hear high-pitched twittering coming from inside the box.

One lunchtime the little inspection door on the front is wide open. I don't like to disturb the birds but I'm concerned that their babies may now be exposed to danger. I climb up the ladder to close it and almost fall off in shock at the sight of the two large grey, featherless birds inside. They are quite hideous, but I suppose their parents must love them. A little later their heads appear at the hole and I can see they have turned pink. I miss their maiden flight and don't see them for a while. Their parents will have taken them to join the flock's group nursery in the paddock over the road.

The orchard is filled with
fragrant pink and white
flowers. Best of all, the
re-grafted Bramleys have a
mass of blossom, delicately
scented and edged with a
stunning deep cherry pink.
This is going to be a good
year. I shall have to do some
serious thinning, but I don't care.
Then one morning, well past the time when the weather bureau issues frost warnings, I wake to find the front paddock crisp and white. I hurry down to the orchard where I check the blossom for damage. The yellow pollen has gone but that may be because the bees have already taken it.

    A week later, tiny apples appear on the trees in the upper rows. In the centre of the orchard the petals have dropped but no fruit has formed. It seems a frosty wind has scythed through the middle rows wiping out all the flowers in its path. It isn't going to be such a large crop after all.

I can't decide whether to mulch the trees or not. A layer of straw would reduce evaporation, but it would also prevent light showers from penetrating the soil. As the spring wears on and rain becomes less frequent, I decide to go ahead. It takes me several days to arrange the straw in a thick layer around each tree. Then we take a short break and spend a weekend at the beach.

    When I return, the straw is no longer where I left it but is now scattered all over the orchard. Only the bottom two rows appear undisturbed. It's there that I find our resident family of choughs. The birds are methodically working their way down the rows, each one tossing straw into the air like a chicken in its search for the insects beneath. I put it all back in place again, but this time

I weight it down with twigs and branches which I drag out of the bush. At this point the choughs seem to lose interest and decide to leave it alone.

Late in the afternoon there's a sudden storm with wild winds and I'm glad I fastened down the straw. Branches are breaking off the gum trees as I hurry into the house. Under the verandah by the back door, there's a small round bird huddled against the wall. It's a button quail. When it doesn't attempt to move away I realise that not only does it need shelter, but is also exhausted.

It huddles beside the door until the storm is over and then disappears. A few weeks later, walking in the bush, I see another quail crossing my path. It's followed by a trail of chicks so tiny I can scarcely believe they are real.

I hear a sudden squeal of pain from the back garden and Reuben, our terrier-cross, comes rushing into the house. The young dog is bleeding profusely from his left ear. A neat V-shaped cut has removed its pointed tip. When I run outside I am just in time to see a blue-tongue lizard march purposefully off into the undergrowth. Reuben won't mess with one again.

If we are to have a crop this year I must find a way to protect the trees before the lorikeets arrive. A nearby orchard is completely enclosed by an enormous tent-like net. I don't think that would be of use here. Besides being too expensive to erect, it would exclude the kangaroos which have always grazed in this paddock in the evenings. In addition, birds could become entangled in the net if they squeezed under its lower edges. I can't imagine myself going down to the orchard every morning to pull out the dead rosellas. Although on paper we own the land, I know we're temporary custodians and have responsibility to do no harm to its plants or wildlife.

It seems best to make a separate net for each tree. After buying the material, I drag it into the spare bedroom where I join the sides together using my old sewing machine. It is weeks of work. Finally I'm ready to cover the first tree, but it's much more difficult than I had imagined. Little spurs catch in the netting and it isn't until most of the apples have been knocked off that I finally succeed.

Eventually I learn to spread the material in a circle on the grass and take hold of its centre before climbing up the ladder. Making sure this point is at the top of the tree, I give a few quick tugs and the net falls like a neat curtain all around. Then I fasten it tightly to the trunk with a large bow, which looks rather silly but is easily undone when there is a need to examine the apples. Now birds can't enter the net from below, and at harvest time any windfalls will be saved from falling to the ground. Soon I become an expert and all alone can net even the largest tree in a few minutes.

At twilight a storm suddenly comes from nowhere. One moment all is calm and at the next a wild violent wind is bending the gum trees and dislodging branches. There is thunder and through the window I see shards of lightning fork across the sky. In a moment driving rain is beating down on the roof. In front of the house I have stacked bags of lime and fertiliser, all that the orchard will need for the next two years. They're covered by a tarpaulin which is held down by a heavy wooden pallet.

As I watch the storm through the window, I see the pallet fly up into the air as if it is weightless, and I know my bags will be ruined. Without further thought I dash outside and find myself wading through a torrent of water flowing through the yard. I have to fight against its strength to force open the side gate. Battling with the wind I catch hold of the tarpaulin before it can blow away, and grasping it in both hands throw myself on top of the pile of bags.

There I lie spread-eagled with the tarpaulin beneath me. The rain that beats down on my skin is needle-sharp and I wonder what I'm doing there. By now I'm completely soaked anyway, so I decide to stay until the rain eases. Fortunately the storm moves on as quickly as it arrived, and after replacing the missing pallet on top of the only slightly wet bags, I make for the house and a hot shower.

Every few days I have to spray the entire orchard against apple scab, a fungal disease that can ruin a whole crop. I don't want to use chemicals to control it, so after some research I decide on an organic lime mixture. I need to cover every apple and both sides of each leaf. With 300 trees to spray it's a slow and fairly exhausting process.

Lime is corrosive and I know I have to wash out the tank and hoses thoroughly. When I have done that at the end of the first morning's spray, I turn my attention to the paintwork, for my red tractor is now a snowy white. I rub and rub, but no matter how hard I try I can't make any impression on the coating of lime, which has baked hard in the sun. None of my soaps and cleaners has any effect, and even a forceful jet from a spray gun does nothing. Finally I drive the tractor back into the shed in despair.

When I take another look at it the next morning, I notice there's no lime around the fill cap where a little diesel has spilled. I don heavy rubber gloves and start working on the paint with a diesel-soaked cloth. Little by little the lime dissolves away. Every morning for a whole week I attack another area until finally I have my beautiful red tractor back again. Next time, before I begin to spray, I wipe diesel all over the paintwork.

I have a problem with my right shoulder. Repeated spraying has made it stiff and sore. The days are warm and humid, ideal for the development of apple scab, so I have no choice but to continue. Nick changes the spraying arrangements and spends several days in the shed working on the new equipment.

Until now I've used a hand-held spray gun. Instead, he fastens nozzles onto a piece of steel attached vertically to the side of the carryall, the platform attached to the back of the tractor that I use to carry the spray tank. This boom is as tall as the apple trees. It can be lowered by removing two screws so the tractor can still fit in the shed. Now all I have to do is sit comfortably on the tractor and crawl slowly along the rows.

In the early morning this works brilliantly, but as often as not a light breeze springs up. When the wind swings around I'm unable to move away from the lime as it blows towards me. By the time I have finished I look like a snowman. Wet weather gear protects my body, but by ten o'clock the plastic suit is making me so hot that it's wetter inside than out, and rivulets of perspiration are running down my legs. Although I wear a beanie to protect my hair, the lime burns the skin on the side of my face. My son makes me a hood from a garbage bag and a plastic visor. It protects me from the lime but after a while it becomes unbearably hot.

The spaces between the rows are wide enough to allow the tractor through, but now the trees are netted I need to drive carefully. Twice the screws on the side of the carryall become caught in a net, and I have to back up and waste time disentangling them. By the time I have finished and stood for half an hour in the hot sun cleaning the tank, I'm completely exhausted and long to put my sweat-soaked body under the shower.

Relieved that the work is finished, I finally drive the tractor into the shed. With a sickening crunch, the still vertical boom smashes into the metal above the doorway and comes crashing down in two pieces. After all Nick's hard work, I can hardly bear to go into the house and break the news.

The following season I decide that shoulder or no shoulder I can't go through this again, and will return to spraying the trees by hand. Nick adds an electric opener to the heavy roller door on the shed, so it opens easily with the press of a button. Amazingly, after this is installed my shoulder pain disappears and despite the hand spraying it doesn't return all season.

We've had a late night, so when I hear the alarm I crawl out of bed only half awake. As I pull open the bedroom curtain, I'm bemused to find myself looking deeply into the eyes of a white horse. For a moment she watches me with friendly interest, before she turns away and begins to eat the weeds in the front garden.

Not long afterwards, as I'm walking up the hill to check the levels in the top dam, I come face to face with a peacock. It must be a female since it doesn't have the male's beautiful long tail feathers. After glancing casually at me, she disappears back into the bush and I never see her again.

Christmas morning, there's a cow happily grazing in the orchard. This land was once part of a dairy farm, and she looks contented. She's a Hereford, having the typical reddish brown body and white curly hair on her face. How she comes to be here I have no idea. As far as I'm aware none of the neighbours has a cow. I am supposed to collect my mother to take her to church for the Christmas morning service, but before I do that I go in search of a rope.

The cow isn't especially afraid of me. I'm able to move quite close to her before she decides she doesn't want to be caught, and takes off at a gallop down the road. I run back to the house and phone the police because I'm afraid she may be hit by a car. My elderly mother, who is late for church, doesn't think much of my excuse that I was trying to catch a cow.

Oliebollen

This recipe will make about ten lovely crisp, fruit-filled doughnuts, traditionally eaten by the Dutch at New Year.

250 millilitres milk
½ packet dried yeast
1 teaspoon caster sugar
½ egg lightly beaten
250 grams flour
1 cooking apple, diced into small pieces
20 grams candied citrus peel
50 grams raisins
pinch salt
oil for deep frying

Heat the milk until just lukewarm. Place the yeast in a small bowl and pour over a little of the warm milk. Stir until yeast has dissolved, then add the sugar. Put the flour into a bowl and make a depression in the centre. Pour in the yeast mixture and add the remaining milk and beaten egg. Stir well.

Add the chopped apple, peel, raisins and salt. Beat the mixture well. Cover the bowl with a damp cloth and leave to rise in a warm place for about an hour or until the mixture has doubled in size.

Heat the oil. Using two metal spoons form the mixture into balls and slip them into the oil a few at a time. Turn occasionally with a slotted spoon. Remove them from the oil when they are a rich brown in colour and put them onto paper towel to drain. Dust with caster sugar.

Appelflappen

This recipe, another favourite at New Year, will make about ten Dutch apple fritters.

½ cup self-raising flour
pinch salt
½ cup milk
¼ cup water
1 lightly beaten egg
2 dessert apples
1 teaspoon caster sugar
ground cinnamon
oil for deep frying

Sift the flour and salt into a bowl and work in the milk, water and egg. Beat until smooth. Leave to stand for about 30 minutes. Beat again. Peel and core the apples and cut them into 1-centimetre rings.

Heat the oil in a deep pan. Using tongs, dip the apple slices into the batter and put them into the hot oil a few at a time. Turn once or twice with a slatted spoon. Remove when nicely browned, checking that the apple inside is cooked.

Drain on paper towel and sprinkle with a mixture of sugar and ground cinnamon. Serve hot.

One day, about to spray a tree, I notice a stick insect on the branch in front of me. It is pale brown and spectacularly long. I have seen these rather comical creatures before, though not in the orchard, and nothing like the size of this giant. Capping my hands around its body, I carefully move it to a tree which has already been sprayed. I'm delighted to have such an interesting animal in the orchard. It only later occurs to me that despite its size, this is not a predator. At this moment it is probably having a hearty lunch of apple leaves. Never mind, how much damage can just one stick insect do?

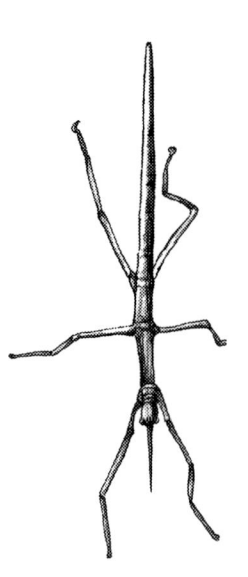

    I normally keep a close watch on the trees so I can deal with any pests as soon as they appear, and before they can spread through the orchard. Occasionally I use pyrethrum, but only when really necessary. In the early spring woolly apple aphids attack the tender bark of the branches. They suck the sap and cause swollen galls to form. Their white cotton-wool appearance makes them easy to spot and I wash them off with soapy water. If I do nothing for a few days, ladybirds suddenly appear on the infested trees to guzzle on them. Their efforts alone, though appreciated, will not be enough to control the pest. Nevertheless I take care to leave enough aphids to make it worthwhile for the ladybirds to remain.

Sometimes when the ants are active there's a larger infestation. The aphids exude honeydew and the ants treat them like miniature cows, milking them for their sweet liquid. They move their tiny herd around the tree, protecting them from predators and seeking out the best places for them to feed.

As summer wears on the temperature rises rapidly, and I have to stop spraying by eleven in the morning or the leaves will burn. So now in order to finish before the forecasted rain, I return to the orchard in the evening. The weather is perfect, with not a breath of wind disturbing the fine mist. The coolness of the night is a welcome relief after the unrelenting heat of the day. Stars fill the sky and above me I can make out the constellation of Orion. After an hour I become bored and turn on my radio, listening to the songs of the sixties as I work, and soon I am dancing to Diana Ross in the moonlight.

One afternoon, on hearing voices, I look up from my weeding in time to see a family with two young children and a bouncy border collie walking along the side of the dam. When they reach the top paddock and begin to throw a stick for the dog, I approach them.

'Can I help you?' I ask politely.

The woman shakes her head briefly and they make to walk on. When I explain that although this may look like open bush it is actually private land, they seem rather offended.

Next day an inspection reveals that the wire on the fence nearest to the recently built houses has rusted. Parts of it are sagging and easily broached. It's time to fix it. Nick buys star posts, strainers and new wire, and with Nat's help, erects a firm new fence. A few days later I spot a young man jogging across the block with a small brown dog at his heels. Examining the new fence I notice that one of the posts has now been deliberately pushed over. Obviously it's impossible to stop really determined trespassers.

Actually, I have mixed feelings about them. As a child in Yorkshire I wandered freely through the fields, climbing over dry-stone walls erected centuries ago. Often there was a little stile, whilst an ancient 'right of way' permitted access to anyone. In summer, families picnicked wherever they wished, setting out checked tablecloths on the grass. As long as they closed the gates after themselves farmers were normally tolerant.

I feel sympathy for the neighbours' children, obliged to play in small neat backyards. They are naturally attracted to our bushland and yabby-filled dams. When, however, I catch two very small boys in gum boots wading in the water, I'm concerned for their safety. After speaking to their parents, my husband mends the fence again and I erect a large NO TRESPASSING sign.

One morning I'm working in the kitchen when the telephone rings. A pleasant female voice tells me she is calling from the BreastScreen clinic, where I have recently had a routine mammogram. There is an instant tightening in my chest. The nurse explains, 'We have found small specks of calcium in your right breast and we would like you to come back to the clinic.'

The panic eases a little as I realise they haven't found a lump, but in my confusion the words come babbling out of my mouth, 'I've had an injury to my right shoulder which probably explains why there might be a build up of calcium.'

The woman listens quietly and then firmly repeats herself. 'You need to come back to the clinic. This is about your breast, not your shoulder.'

It's on my birthday, almost a month since the first phone call, that I am finally diagnosed with invasive breast cancer. After the operation my prognosis is good, but I don't return to work in the orchard for a long time. Physically I make a satisfactory recovery but I'm beset by fears and depressive thoughts.

Then one day, wandering aimlessly between the rows of apple trees, I fail to notice the rising wind and darkening skies. Suddenly the rain comes down heavily and I know that before I can make it back to the house I shall be soaked. Two rows away there is a Beauty of Bath with spreading branches and I run to shelter under its thick green canopy. Raindrops bounce off the leaves and an occasional drop of moisture hits the warm skin of my bare arms, but mostly I remain dry. Crouching down among the roots I breathe in the sweet musky smell of the rich brown soil, darkening in the rain. It makes me think of a workmate who, when suffering a bout of anxiety and depression, was told by her counsellor to take off her shoes, go outside, and rub her feet into the bare earth. I watch the rain for a while, peering through the moist leaves, until the wind drops suddenly and the squall is over. It's time to start work again amongst the trees.

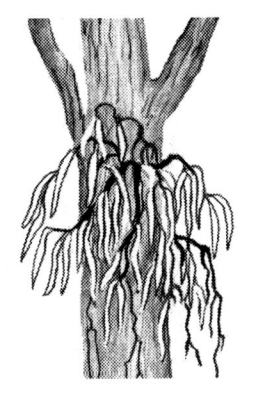

There are two parasites on our block. A large bouquet of mistletoe grows on the red box tree behind the house and it is visited regularly by the tiny mistletoe bird. I know he's around when I hear his high-pitched, warbling song. He is a glossy blue-black with a white chest and a flash of bright red at his throat. Unlike other birds, he deposits his droppings directly onto the branch on which he's resting, allowing the sticky mistletoe seed to send out its tendrils into the wood.

The cherry ballart bush takes its nutrients from the roots of a gum tree. Its red, cherry-like fruits are popular with the birds and can be eaten by humans apparently, although I haven't dared to try them.

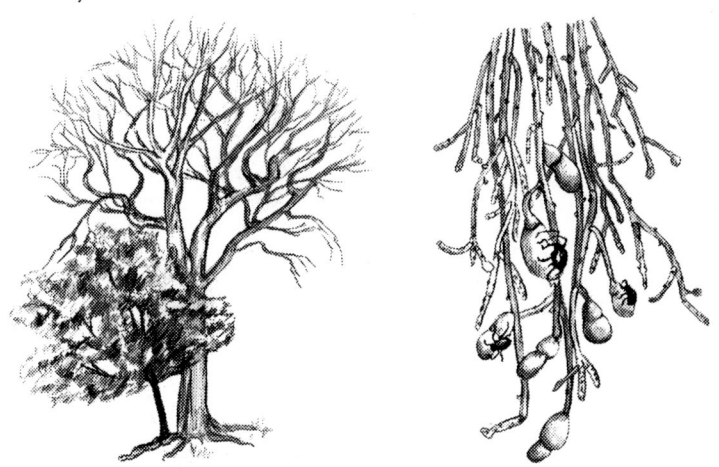

When I was a young girl in Yorkshire, I climbed into my grandfather's tree and dropped the apples down to where my mother waited to catch them in her apron. They were big green apples and two would be enough for a pie. I was never tempted to bite into them because they were as sour as a lemon.

Bramleys are true 'cookers', their strong acidity giving a wonderful flavour to any pie or crumble. They're unusual in that when cooked, they turn to a yellow fluff that needs no breaking up with a fork. Cored, stuffed with brown sugar and raisins and then baked whole in the oven, they are a delicacy. In my grandparents' house, the Bramleys were arranged on a stone slab in the cellar in long neat rows. There they remained firm throughout the winter months, always available for a pie or sauce to be served with the Sunday roast.

Baked Apples

This recipe is good with Granny Smiths but wonderful with Bramleys, which change to a yellow fluff.

Wash and core 1 cooking apple per person (but do not peel).
Spoon the filling of brown sugar, a little chopped butter, a few raisins and/or flaked almonds into the apple cavities.
Place the apples in a deep dish. Cover with foil and bake in a 200°C oven for about 30 minutes. Use a skewer to check that the centre of the apple is soft.

Bacon and Apple Slice

2 sheets of frozen shortcrust pastry
2 medium onions
125 grams free-range bacon
1 cooking apple, peeled and cored
oil and margarine for frying
1 tablespoon French mustard (or more according to taste)
milk

Partly thaw the pastry. Place one piece on a greased baking sheet. Chop the onions, apple and bacon into small pieces. Melt a little margarine and oil in a large frying pan and add all three ingredients, cooking gently until soft and golden brown. Stir in the mustard.

Turn out onto centre of sheet of pastry. Using a brush dampen the pastry edges with a little milk and place second sheet on top. Cut off the excess pastry at the corners. Press the edges together, then crimp up. If desired, shape the spare pieces of pastry into leaves for decoration. Brush top with milk. Chill in fridge for a few minutes. Then cook at 170°C for approx. 15 minutes until pastry is nicely browned. Remove from oven, cut in slices and serve at once.

Apple Dumplings

An easy dessert, lovely on a cold night.

For each person —
1 cooking apple
1 square of either shortcrust or puff pastry, large enough to enclose an apple
1 teaspoon brown sugar
2 or 3 dried apricots
few chopped hazelnuts or flaked almonds
knob of butter
pinch of cinnamon
milk
a little beaten egg

Peel and core the apples and mix together the other ingredients to fill each apple cavity.

Place each apple in the centre of a pastry square. Draw up the edges of the pastry around the apple, brush the edges with milk and press together to seal well. Trim excess pastry and turn the apples over so that the pastry joins are underneath. Use the leftover pastry to make a leaf for decoration.

Place apples on a baking sheet lined with nonstick paper and bake at 200°C/180°C fan-forced for about 30 minutes.

As my Bramley apples mature in the summer heat, I notice they don't have the slightly oval, flattened shape that I remember from my childhood. A few weeks later their green colour gives way to a pale yellow and they develop a faint apricot blush. I pick an apple and bite into it, anticipating a rush of strong acidic flavour. Instead I have a mouthful of bland, uninteresting flesh.

Of the 300 trees we've planted, 120 are going to produce a crop of pale, insipid apples. I am bitterly disappointed. Of course the apples I remember grew in the relatively cool summers of northern England. Perhaps the reason why people don't grow Bramleys in Australia is because they don't do well in a hot climate.

We bought the trees from Clive and Margaret, so I give them a call. They're interested in seeing our first fruit, and come to look at the orchard. As we wander along the rows of Bramleys we're drawn to a tree quite different from the rest. This one is wide and spreading and on its branches are hung the flat green apples of my childhood. Puzzled, we walk on and discover two more trees which have produced 'true' Bramley apples. It is then we realise there has been a mistake. Of the 120 trees we bought as Bramley's Seedling only three actually are Bramleys. The remainders are of an unknown variety Clive and Margaret have never seen before, and which Clive now christens a 'pseudo-Bram'.

They are both horrified, not only because of this particular disaster, but also because Bramleys have been their best-selling variety for years. In the time it's taken for my trees to grow fruit, they may have mistakenly sold pseudo-Brams to a host of other people. There could be all kinds of repercussions. I feel terribly sorry for them, especially since it wasn't their mistake. It seems they purchased the bud wood from Tasmania where the mix

Pseudo-Bram

up must have occurred. The three true Bramleys would have come from their own Bramley tree.

At least I have the compensation of knowing good Bramleys can actually be grown in this climate. I'm also relieved to know that these pale tasteless apples are not the result of any orchard mismanagement on my part. Immediately Clive offers to re-graft all the pseudo-Brams, turning them back into true Bramleys. I can scarcely believe this is possible, but sure enough, he arrives in the winter carrying his pruning saw. He proceeds to remove the limbs from the trees, in some cases leaving only a trunk.

In the early spring he returns, this time bearing long bundles of brown twigs ready to be grafted onto the now denuded trees. The sap has risen and it's time to begin. Clive gently eases the spoon shaped blade of his pruning knife between the bark and the green wood within. He selects a cutting with thick buds and slices it diagonally to create a fine flat point. Then he makes a slit in the branch of the tree and slides the twig firmly beneath the bark. He binds it tightly in place before giving the graft a waterproof coating.

Clive comes every morning for three weeks and together we work our way along the rows of pseudo-Brams. He tries to teach me his skills but I'm not very good at grafting. Eventually he gives up and just hands me the paintbrush. As we work he tells me fascinating stories of the time when he was an actor. Mostly though, we talk about apple trees, for we both share an abiding love for them. In no time there are green leaves on our little twigs, and mere trunks have become growing trees again. The following spring he returns and we repeat the effort until they are all fully limbed.

Water trickles over the rim of an earthenware pot in the back garden. Thornbills, wrens and pardalotes drink and bathe there. Frogs and small lizards live amongst the damp rocks at its base.

With so much land clearance and building in the surrounding area, many breeding sites for birds have been destroyed. Last season we fastened nesting boxes onto two small gum trees in the front orchard. Although it might seem strange for an apple grower to encourage parrots, the fruit is protected by nets now and they can do no harm.

Two eastern rosellas come on a daily basis to inspect the boxes. Before they begin to breed this year I do a check and discover the box they occupied last year has a rotting base. Although the other one is in good condition the birds have never paid it any attention. Perhaps it's in a position they don't like.

I enlist the help of my son Nathaniel, who climbs up the ladder and takes down the damaged box. We plan to replace it with the good, unused one from the other tree, so he takes this one down also. Before he goes back up the ladder, I open the little inspection door in the front of the box to make sure there's no debris inside. Here are two blue feathers from a rosella's tail at the edge of a neat little nest of gum leaves. As I look, a sugar glider suddenly flies out of the door and runs up my son's leg, before leaping into the branches of the tree above us. We turn to each other in shock.

Feeling guilty for disturbing the poor little creature's sleep, we quickly return the box to its original position. The next day I gingerly open the inspection door to see if our friend has returned and I'm rewarded with the sight of a little pink nose. All is well.

One morning I discover a brown snake caught in a net which was left lying at the edge of the orchard after we picked the apples. Immediately I feel guilty. It's my net, my fault. What can I do? Anyone I call in to help will knock it on the head with a spade. I could just walk away, but I wouldn't be able to sleep at night knowing the poor thing is trapped and slowly starving to death. I go to look for my sewing scissors.

The snake lies perfectly still. Maybe it's dead. I slip the scissors between nylon and scale and carefully cut into a few layers of netting. The tail suddenly whips around and I leap out of the way. But when I look again I see that the snake's head is so hopelessly entangled it can't possibly bite me. Soon I manage to free the body. It is a beautiful, warm brown creature and its little bright eyes look up at me pleadingly.

I know this is madness, but how can I leave it now? In its struggle to escape, the nylon has tightened around the arrow-shaped head, and it's difficult to force in the points of my scissors without harming the skin. As the last strand comes free I prepare to jump for my life, but the snake doesn't move. Then slowly, its jaws part and I can see its soft pink gums. The snake continues to hold its mouth wide open, almost as if it's trying to show me something.

Gingerly creeping forward, I discover a last strand of nylon wrapped around a tooth. I pause. Until now I've been lucky, but doing dental work on a brown snake is a bit much. Its tiny button eyes gaze into mine. I've been very gentle and somehow I know it's aware I'm trying to help. It isn't going to bite me. Still, I don't want it to kill me by accident, so I find a longish, thin stick and carefully lift the last strand from around the tooth.

There are a few sudden contortions. For a moment its eyes catch mine, before it quietly turns away and sets off down to the dam to look for frogs.

I'm sitting on the verandah reading, when I hear barking. I look over the fence and see Reuben up near the top dam. He's chasing a fox. When I call out to him he turns back towards the house, but instead of making its escape, the fox follows the little dog down the hill. As soon as he notices, he chases it up the paddock again, and the game continues back and forth until at last the fox tires of it and disappears into the bush.

Reuben's a funny little dog. Sometimes he steps on a sharp twig or thorn when we're out walking. At once he runs back on three legs and holds up the injured foot to show me. Usually there's no splinter in it and no damage done. Still, I rub it anyway and tell him he's all right. At once he looks relieved and trots away on four legs again. It reminds me of all those times I cured my children of bumps and scratches just by kissing them better.

When we go out for the day we leave our dogs indoors. They're well behaved and don't make a mess. That is, except for one occasion when we came home very late. As I walked into the living room I noticed the wooden kava bowl on the coffee table was full of water. No, not water. Reuben wouldn't have liked to ruin the carpet, so when he grew desperate he must have searched for the nearest equivalent to a toilet.

He's always by my side. When I'm working along the rows in the orchard he lies quietly under a nearby apple tree and appears to be asleep. I find though, that once the distance between us is more than three trees he has to get up and move close to me again.

I've noticed he feels responsible for the other dogs. At times he'll paw at my leg and insist I follow him to the door, where a very cold chihuahua will be waiting to be let inside.

Often when my husband is away on business I stay up late reading. Reuben sleeps beside me, but some time after midnight he makes it perfectly clear that I should be in bed. He won't leave me alone until I put my book away and head for the bathroom.

He's twelve now and his heart's failing. Fluid is building in his lungs and he can't walk very far. The vet says it won't be long.

I have a feeling Reuben knows, but he still greets every day with joy. He delights in simple things: his walk, an interesting smell, a tickle under his chin and a few loving words whispered in his ear at bedtime. He watches over me. I shall miss him.

The branches of the apple trees have become compacted and tangled, so Clive comes again to show me how to prune them. He stands back and observes the tree for some time. He walks slowly around, bending down first one branch and then another. I can't imagine what he's looking at. There are dozens of trees to be worked on and this is taking far too long. I am sure there are rules about pruning. Why can't he just tell me what they are so I can get on with it?

Then as I watch and listen, I begin to understand how every tree is different and develops in its own unique way. Damaged or crossed branches need to be removed. One tree grows too densely; another needs branches tying down to achieve a satisfactory shape. It's a matter of balance and developing a 'feel' for the tree. Once you have that, pruning becomes an easy task. After a while I'm usually in agreement with Clive as to which branches to cut. As my confidence grows I enjoy pruning more and more, and eventually it becomes my favourite work in the orchard.

For some reason the Belle de Boskoops refuse to flower. I search through my books for an explanation and discover that fruiting normally occurs on horizontal boughs. To encourage flower formation the more upright ones should be weighed down. With that in mind, I set to work on my machine sewing dozens of little calico bags, which I fill with gravel. Then I spend a day hanging them in the trees so the branches are nicely flattened.

The following year there is still no fruit. I look at the Tydeman's Early Worcesters growing between the Belle be Boskoops. They are full of apples carried on branches which shoot almost vertically towards the sky. It's time for further research. Eventually, on a Dutch web site, I read that Belles are notoriously slow to mature and can take up to twelve years before they produce fruit. It seems a likely explanation, but I'm not exactly thrilled, since it means we may still have another three years to wait for their apples.

There's an enormous web strung between two rows of trees. It's been made by a golden orb weaver spider who sits motionless in its centre, waiting for her prey. Her body is silver grey and her long slender legs are striped with red. The web glistens in the sunlight for it's made of golden thread. It's so strong that when I pull it with my finger it doesn't break. Fortunately for the spider I only drive the tractor down every second row when I'm spraying, so I won't have to disturb her.

There are many smaller spiders hidden within the apple trees. Their papery golden egg sacs hang down in strings from the branches. I need to protect the trees from apple scab, but I try to avoid spraying directly onto the spiders. As I begin, the larger ones scuttle into the dark security of the tree guards and the smaller ones leap out into space, hanging on silken thread from the boughs until I've finished.

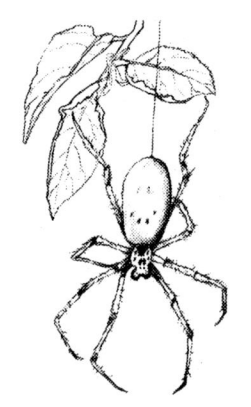

It's autumn and time to pick the fruit. Les comes to help me. We untie the first net and start to ease it free of the branches. It has to be done carefully because the apples are ready to drop and any shaking will dislodge them. As we lift the net a fine cloud of powdered lime is released into the air around us. We catch our breath and our eyes begin to smart. I go in search of masks and goggles hoping these will solve the problem, but the goggles soon mist up inside and become obscured on the outside by the dust. This is going to be a horrible job.

The apples all have a white coating which has to be removed before they can be sold. I work for days and days at the sink in the shed, brushing each apple clean. When finally they are all shiny and beautiful, I weigh them and pack them into boxes, ready to be sold.

Once the apples are picked the trees have a further spurt of growth, but by June the bare branches are surrounded by brown leaves rotting on the ground. It's on these leaves that the spores of apple scab remain dormant over winter. When the spring rains hit them they will re-infect next season's leaves and fruit. Every year seems to be dryer than the last and although the trees are irrigated, higher temperatures and the changing weather patterns are making them more vulnerable to the disease.

Having had two outbreaks of scab during the season despite all my spraying, I resolve to remove as many of the infected leaves as possible. They have to be raked from around the trees, piled into mounds and then carted off to the tip. It's backbreaking work and takes me a whole week. When spring comes again and there are fresh signs of scab, I decide the effort just wasn't worthwhile. Next year I shall let the leaves remain where they fall and perhaps bury them under a layer of mulch instead.

PART THREE

Drought

It's been eleven years since we planted the orchard and every year has been drier than the last. Now the people of Bendigo are forced to use bath water on their plants and succulents and cacti have replaced hollyhocks and pansies.

Because of the drought the water authority has reduced our allocation by two-thirds, so now it will be a struggle to keep the trees alive. I have seen council workers dig slotted agricultural pipe into the ground when planting street trees. The irrigation water goes directly to the roots so there's little loss from evaporation. If I can do this in the orchard it could save a large amount of water.

First I need 300 holes. I enlist Les's help and he comes with me to hire a post-hole digger, since I wouldn't recognise one if I saw it. The hole needs to be a good fit for the pipe, so we test out a machine in the hire company's yard, making quite a large hole. Fortunately nobody seems to notice. I cut up the pipe and Les drags the digger into the orchard.

We quickly discover we have a problem. The council workers dig the hole before they plant the tree. Our trees are fully grown and many of them have low spreading branches. This makes it extremely difficult to move the digger close enough to make a hole near the roots. Because the trees were planted on mounds, we have to push the heavy machine uphill. Each tree is different and Les struggles to manoeuvre the ungainly device this way and that, whilst I push the branches out of his way. A lesser man would have thrown in the sponge but Les, with his endless patience, perseveres and eventually there's a neat hole close to every tree. I drop in the lengths of pipe, adjust the drippers, and declare the operation a success.

Despite the drought and heat, the magpies manage to raise two noisy babies. They stay close to the house where there is plenty of water. When the dog falls asleep they're onto her bone in a flash.

The paddocks are bare. By piping the water below ground, we've reduced the grass growing around the apple trees, so there's little now for the hungry kangaroos to eat. They begin to attack the plums and damage shrubs they have never touched before. In the early evening, the boldest of them comes right into the front garden to drink from the birdbath. There's so little feed remaining that I am afraid they may die.

I put out a trough of water beside the orchard and buy them a bale of lucerne hay. Every evening five or six kangaroos file down the hill from the bush where they have sheltered from the hot sun during the day, to congregate around the trough. They take it in turns to drink, the big male exercising his right to go first.

He seems to take a long time to have his fill, dipping his head down to the water again and again. When the patience of one of the younger males wears thin, he approaches but is quickly driven away. Yet when the young joey comes close, his father stands aside to allow him to drink.

I have to pass close to the trough on my way to turn off the irrigation in the evening. Walking slowly, I turn my face away from the kangaroos and act as if I haven't noticed they are there. At first they hop away when I approach, but soon they become used to my nightly walks and only look up briefly as I pass by. Sometimes visitors would like to see the kangaroos 'up close'. They follow me into the orchard but are only rewarded with a brief glance before the animals make a break for the bush. It's as if all the members of the little mob know me personally and understand I'll do them no harm.

Late one hot afternoon I'm wandering through the bush behind the house when my path is crossed by a long procession of hairy caterpillars, following each other nose to tail. Some distance away I see those at the head of the line begin to climb the trunk of a wattle tree.

A cloud of butterflies hovers over the yellow everlasting flowers. They appear to be two different species but are actually all common browns. The females are a little different from the males, having darker markings on their wingtips.

There is a commotion in the bush. All around me birds are calling out in alarm. Then just ahead I spot a wedge-tailed eagle, improbably perched on the lowest branch of a small gum tree. I can't imagine what it can be doing there. Perhaps it has become exhausted by the heat. It stays on the same tree for nearly an hour before it recovers and flies away.

In some seasons there's a mouse problem. Perhaps it has something to do with the weather. Suddenly, the shopping baskets at the Coles supermarket are carrying the telltale little traps tossed on top of the vegetables and groceries. The mice always manage to get into the roof cavity, and it's when I turn over in bed at night that I first hear their furtive scurrying. We should do something about the problem immediately, but of course, being slack, we don't.

In no time a tiny mouse is visiting us in the evening when we are watching television. It boldly patters across the slate floor, giving the slumbering dogs a wide berth. This is such a perfect, neatly made little creature. Of course this can't continue and Nick speaks warningly of the need for poisons and other unspeakables.

Still, aware of my sensitivities, he arrives home from shopping next day carrying a blue plastic 'humane' mouse trap. All we have to do is put a small piece of cheese or chocolate on a spike inside. When the mouse takes the bait a door drops down and catches it unharmed. The label offers various suggestions for disposal of the caught animal, but all of them are unpalatable as far as I'm concerned. We do have a large block of land, however, so when I hear the trapdoor click I set out with a torch and carry the box all the way to our fence line. There, pointing the little fellow in the general direction of the newly emerging housing estate at our border, I release him into the bush.

For a few nights Nick watches without comment as I leave the house bearing yet another mouse. Then he suggests I paint a white spot on the back of the next one before I let it go, because he suspects the mice are making it back before me. Finally, when they begin to eat the soap in the bathroom I give in and Nick calls the pest exterminator.

Then one evening, when semi-comatose we loll in front of the television, a sudden sound from the kitchen jolts us awake. There's a shockingly loud scratching sound coming from the ceiling above the corner cupboard. We look at each other wondering what kind of large animal could be making so much noise, before coming to the conclusion there must be a possum in the roof cavity.

I have looked for possums and been disappointed that although we have the little sugar gliders, there are no signs of ringtails or brushtails living on our block. Of course having a large possum in the roof cavity is no cause for celebration. We have both heard dire tales of nightly scratching, shrieking and urine dripping down from above. Nick grabs a kitchen spatula and making a huge row, bashes it repeatedly on the ceiling.

Afterwards we wait expectantly for the scratching sounds to resume but now there is only silence. Two weeks later we hear the noises again. This time we know what to do, and soon all is peaceful.

Some days later we are busy preparing for a formal dinner party. I set places for twelve people around two tables on the verandah. Each one is covered with a crisp white tablecloth and decorated with vases of cream roses. I have made sherry trifle and Nick, who is a wonderful chef, has prepared an array of splendid casseroles and curries.

It's a perfect, balmy summer evening, and after our guests have eaten the main course I light the candles in the gathering twilight. The hum of conversation grows as our guests relax and enjoy their wine and trifle. As I lean back in my chair, I suddenly catch sight of a large rat running across a beam of the pergola just above our heads. It disappears under the eaves. A moment later it reappears, running along the beam in the opposite direction.

Horrified, I glance around at the guests, who seem undisturbed, but catching my husband's eye I realise that he's also spotted the rat. Mute, I wait in anticipation for the sudden outcry and panic. None comes, and for the rest of the evening I struggle to ignore the frequent comings and goings overhead. Next day we buy rat poison.

English Sherry Trifle

The recipe for this sumptuous trifle was given to me many years ago by a Yorkshire lady, Joan Watson. In her nineties now, she's still a wonderful cook

150 grams sponge cake
120 millilitres sweet sherry (or to taste)
825 grams can of fruit salad
(or other soft fruit such as berries)
85 grams port wine jelly
150 millilitres boiling water
60 grams custard powder
550 millilitres milk
2 tablespoons caster sugar
40 grams lightly toasted flaked almonds
300 millilitres thickened cream
1 teaspoon vanilla essence
6 glacé cherries

Slice the cake and place in the bottom of a large glass bowl. Drench with the sherry. Drain the juice from the fruit and set aside. Put the fruit on top of the cake.

Make the jelly using the boiling water. Stir until the crystals have dissolved and then use the fruit juice to make it up to 400 millilitres, and pour it over the fruit.

Dissolve the custard powder in 100 millilitres of the cold milk and stir in the sugar. Heat the remaining 450 millilitres of milk until almost boiling. Pour over the custard and quickly return to the pan. Stir over a low heat until it thickens, and then remove it from the heat. Cover the surface with plastic wrap to prevent a skin from forming.

Place almonds under grill until lightly browned. When the custard is cold spoon it into the bowl, forming a layer over the set jelly. Whip the cream until stiff and then gently stir in the vanilla essence. Place a blanket of cream over the custard. Arrange cherries on the top and sprinkle the almonds around the edge.

Dutch Apple Cake

This unusual cake is brimming with apples.

Pastry
185 grams butter
75 grams caster sugar
1 egg yolk
200 grams flour
1 dessertspoon iced water
finely grated rind of 1 large lemon
few drops vanilla essence

Filling
5–6 large cooking apples
½ cup sugar
ground cinnamon
handful of raisins or mixed dried fruit
25 grams flaked almonds

Cream butter and sugar. Stir in the egg yolk and add the flour, water, lemon rind and vanilla essence. Mix with hands. Chill for 30 minutes.

Divide the pastry into 2 portions, one slightly larger than the other. Press larger portion into base and sides of a greased 20-centimetre springform cake tin. Chill.

Peel, core and thickly slice the apples and put into pastry case, lightly sprinkling the layers with sugar, cinnamon and raisins. Roll out remaining pastry onto a floured board. Cut into strips and arrange on top of apples in a lattice pattern. Sprinkle top of cake with cinnamon and flaked almonds.

Bake in a hot oven for 30 minutes then reduce to moderate and bake for a further 30–45 minutes until apples are tender and pastry is golden. Leave in tin until cool. Remove and serve with cream.

Coffee Hazelnut Cake

This is actually a rich dessert somewhat similar to tiramisu.

175 grams butter or margarine
175 grams caster sugar
3 eggs, lightly beaten
175 grams self-raising flour
3 tablespoons instant coffee
425 millilitres water
225 grams caster sugar
2 tablespoons brandy
275 grams thickened cream
1 teaspoon vanilla essence
30 grams dry-roasted unsalted hazelnuts

Cream the butter and sugar together until light and fluffy. Gradually beat in the eggs. Sift the flour and fold into the mixture. Turn into a greased and lined 20-centimetre cake tin. Bake in a preheated oven at 180°C for about 45 minutes. Test with a skewer near the end of cooking.

Meanwhile, dissolve the powdered coffee in 100 millilitres of the water. Place the remaining water and the sugar in a pan. Heat it gently until the sugar has dissolved and then simmer until a light syrup forms. Remove from the heat and add the coffee and brandy.

When the cake is cooked remove from the oven and place on a deep dish. Pierce it all over with a skewer and pour the warm coffee mixture over the hot cake. Leave to stand overnight.

Next day whip the cream and vanilla essence and use to coat the cake. Roughly chop the hazelnuts and sprinkle them around the edge.

For the first time a black wallaby comes out of the bush to drink from the birdbath, thirst overcoming his shyness. Whilst in the front garden he makes short work of my roses. Knowing he'll return, I dig them up and put them in pots on the back verandah.

A massive bushfire is raging in the hill country. It's many kilometres from here yet the smoke is dense in the orchard, making work impossible. Repeated lime sprays have whitened the trees and in the swirling mistiness they are strange, ethereal. I think of snowy Christmases in England.

A pair of plovers has moved into the orchard. The birds run about searching for grubs in the moist earth around the tree roots. Oddly, for they're not nocturnal, I hear their anxious warning call late into the night. Perhaps a fox startles them. They disappear for a while in the spring but then return, bringing two fledglings with them. I watch the family carefully for I've seen plovers viciously attacking anyone approaching their young. Luckily, they seem to realise they're just guests in the orchard and move politely out of the way when I come too close.

At night when I'm lying in my bed
I can hear the eerie call of the tawny
frogmouth. The soft *boom boom* is repeated
over and over like the sound of a distant
lighthouse warning ships in the fog.
He's a strange bird, with a massive mouth.
At night he hunts like an owl and in the
daytime he sits in the fork of a tall gum
tree near the gate. With his pale mottled
feathers and outstretched bill he's almost
indistinguishable from the branches of
the tree.

It's a stifling hot day and I struggle home with my shopping. At the back door I fumble in my handbag for the house keys and in so doing, let drop the grocery bag. It narrowly misses a small dark snake curled up on the doormat. I freeze, and for a few moments we stare at each other. Then the little whip-like creature glides around my feet and disappears into the undergrowth.

The garden is wilting in the heat. As I begin to water a pink daisy bush, a tiny jewel-like pardalote flutters into its centre to catch the cool spray. It's only as far away as the length of my arm.

Raw Herring Salad

In the very hot weather when we don't feel like cooking, these two appley salads make a refreshing meal.

250 gram packet of matjes herring fillets
4 hard-boiled eggs
2 green apples, peeled, cored
1 medium beetroot
1 small onion
4 medium gherkins
3 medium potatoes, cooked
3 tablespoons olive oil
2 tablespoons white vinegar
¼ teaspoon salt
pepper
mayonnaise
lettuce leaves
sprig of parsley

Remove herrings from the packet and soak in cold water for an hour, changing the water once to reduce the oil and salt. Cut the fillets into pieces.

Slice two hard-boiled eggs and set aside, together with a few small pieces of herring. Chop the apples, beetroot, onion, gherkins and potatoes and mix together in a bowl. Chop the remaining eggs into pieces and add them to the bowl. Add the herring, reserving a few pieces for decoration. Stir in the vinegar, olive oil, salt and pepper.

Turn the contents of the bowl onto a large plate. Use a spatula to press the mixture into a mounded shape. Cover this with mayonnaise and arrange a few lettuce leaves around the edge. Decorate with the egg slices, remaining herring pieces and a little chopped parsley.

Witlof and Anchovy Salad

2 hard-boiled eggs
English salad cream (or mayonnaise)
8 anchovy fillets
1 head of witlof
1 green apple
small piece of onion
1 teaspoon lemon juice
salt and pepper

Slice eggs in half lengthways and place in centre of a plate yolk down. Coat with salad cream and arrange anchovy strips over them. Slice the witlof, apples and onion. Mix together with the lemon juice, salt and pepper and a little salad cream. Arrange around the eggs.

Coby our German shorthaired pointer is my constant companion in the orchard. But when she turns fifteen, dementia sets in, so we have to call the vet and say a loving farewell. We have already adopted a two-year-old English springer spaniel named Morgan and now she, too, follows me into the orchard. Sadly we don't have her long.

One lunchtime we return from shopping to find that she is ill and vomiting repeatedly. At first glance it appears to be a stomach upset but when she begins to shake and lose the use of her legs, we rush her to the vet. He tells us she has been poisoned by something quite deadly; most probably snail bait.

The vet puts her on a drip before sending us home to try to discover what she has eaten. We don't use poisons in the garden so I can't think what she could have found, but in amongst the revolting pools of vomit I see the black feathers of a bird. Less than an hour later the vet calls to tell us he couldn't save her. It is heartbreaking and unexpected, and I now wish I had stayed with her. She was a lovely young dog, and she suffered horribly.

Two days later, there's a dead chough in the middle of the driveway. It's a strange place for a bird to die. There are no marks on its body. Then a little distance away underneath a small wattle bush, I discover a second dead chough. The next time I hear the familiar whistling I look for the other members of the family. Only three of the nine birds are left. They must have been feeding in some distant garden and eaten snail pellets.

Sadly Morgan had a habit of chewing on anything interesting she discovered in the bush. It seems that by finding and eating one of the dead choughs she's become another victim. If only gardeners would use some of the simple organic ways available to keep snails from their vegetable plots.

As yet there have been no summer thunderstorms to refill the dams. Despite last year's effort to deliver water directly to the roots, the orchard is suffering from a lack of moisture. Still I'm convinced the drought will end soon and the rains will return as they always have in the past. I just have to keep the trees alive until then.

As the weather grows hotter and water becomes scarce, I move as many plants as possible into the shade of the verandah. They attract both butterflies and dragonflies. When these become trapped by the shadecloth overhead, they make easy pickings for the pardalotes and fairy wrens.

The drought is interminable and all around life is struggling for survival. Dead branches are dropping from the gum trees. The bush is strangely silent, bereft of birds. In Ouyen, desperate farmers' wives perform a naked rain dance, as the soil in the paddocks turns to dust and blows away on the wind.

We're eating outside, our food illuminated by candlelight, when joy of joys, we feel the first drops of rain. Soon it's falling steadily but no one moves to go inside. It's been so long since we felt its gentle touch on our warm skin. A fat brown frog appears from nowhere and nonchalantly hops across the dinner table before disappearing into the undergrowth.

In the morning the wrens and silvereyes return, joyfully calling out to each other as they search for the newly emerging insects in the gum trees. Water has run into the dams during the night, and the apple trees have had a thorough soaking. A few days later the kangaroos are feasting on tender new shoots of grass. But this is only a temporary respite. Within two weeks the sun has done its work and beneath cloudless blue skies, the soil returns to dust.

The Tydeman's Early Worcesters are almost ready for picking and the skins of the Autumn Pearmains are showing their characteristic deep-orange stripes. During the night the temperature remains high as the heat wave continues. It is unusually hot, even for January in Bendigo. The thermometer, nailed to a fence post at the corner of the orchard, registers forty-two degrees. Despite frequent watering, the leaves on the rose bushes turn black and when I touch them they crumble into dust.

Now the apples are changing colour and I realise the fruit is actually cooking on the trees. Even those growing in deep shade have been affected. In past years there has been some fruit spoilt by sunburn but I've never seen anything like this. The whole crop is ruined. Months of pruning, thinning and spraying have come to nothing.

At the end of a long night's foraging, the kangaroos stop for a while in front of the house to stretch, clean, and scratch.

Then they go to sit in the shade below the far dam, before finally falling asleep amongst the yellow everlasting flowers.

Two of the dams are dry and only the one above the orchard still contains water. Tall reeds have grown in its centre, making it impossible to see how much remains. Presently I am running the irrigation for the trees at six day intervals. The water runs slowly into the buried pipes, gently spreading underground to reach the thirsty roots. I have a water meter with a prong which I insert into the soil to test for moisture, so I don't give the trees a drop more than they need.

Now the question is – how many more times can I irrigate with these last dregs of water? The answer is probably only twice, which means that unless it rains very soon the trees will begin to dry out and die.

A week later it still hasn't rained and I'm losing hope. Instead of putting on the usual amount of water, I'm now rationing the trees to a few brief minutes at a time. This is not good for them but I'm finding it hard to face the moment when the dam runs dry. Twice a day I go to the computer, scanning two different websites to check the forecast. This constant monitoring is of course pointless and I know it's becoming neurotic. I need a miracle, preferably in the form of a big storm, but I'll happily settle for a few showers to see the trees through another week. No rain is forecast.

There's nothing more I can do except leave the block for a while and think about something else, so I drive into the town and wander around the shops. At lunchtime I return, swinging my car into the small dirt road beside our property. As I do so I hear a loud rushing sound. A great torrent of water is bursting out of the bush and madly, wildly, heading towards our dam.

This isn't the gentle flow of irrigation water, nor even what happens during a storm. This is an amazing thundering river coming from nowhere, surreal in the parched landscape. I drive onto our block and run down to the dam. In half an hour it will be overflowing.

Some distance away in the bush the irrigation channel passes under a small road, and I set off at a jog through the trees to see the origin of this miracle. The concrete channel has never been more than half full, but now its steep sides are hidden by a wall of water which is pouring into the bush. A dry walking track between the gum trees has been transformed into a rushing river.

For some time I have scarcely heard a bird sing. The little blue wrens that so merrily hopped around our front garden are long gone, driven away by the drought and lack of insect life. Now above the noise of the running water I hear their excited twitter. I return to the house to somewhat reluctantly do the right thing and telephone the water authority. There is as much water now in the bottom dam as we have received in our entire allocation for the year. The orchard will survive.

In the evening the sound is amazing as dozens of frogs make love calls to each other. I stand beside the bottom dam in the moonlight listening to them. One sounds as if a saw is cutting back and forth through a log. Then there is an interrupted *creak* . . . *creak*. Between the sawing and creaking I hear the full-throated, intermittent *bonk* . . . *bonk* of the pobblebonk frog, and a classic *rivet* . . . *rivet* echoes from the far bank.

The frogs have dug deep down into the mud at the bottom of the dam in order to escape from the heat of the hot summer. They have been silent for a long time. I am happy to hear them again and know they have survived the drought.

A constant stream of birds comes to the water fountain. In the searing heat they hold their beaks wide open as if they are gasping for breath. A currawong strides through the bushes before perching on the side of the bowl. Even though he must be desperate for a drink, he's nervous. He looks this way and that for several minutes, checking and re-checking for predators, before finally dipping his beak into the cool clear water.

There's no feed in the paddocks and few insects in the trees, so everywhere animals are parched and hungry. There are all kinds of native plants in the front garden, put there to attract the birds, but there are no flowers and there's no food in them now.

Nick hangs a bird feeder on the front verandah. I fill it and scatter seed on the ground below. In no time there are a dozen birds coming to eat there, including a lame duck and a one-eyed magpie. Ducks rule, chasing away the crested pigeons and magpies until they have finished. The shy bronzewing pigeons have to wait for the leftovers, but the eastern rosellas avoid the fight by using the feeder. Because of its overhanging roof, it's impossible for the birds to access the seed from above and they need to land directly onto the base. The rosellas have no difficulty with this and nor do the crested pigeons. Our two resident galahs, however, alight over and over again on the roof, and with one claw grasping the chain try without success to slide down to the seed. After a week they figure it out.

A flock of galahs lives in the paddock across the road, and periodically these birds also come to the feeder. They take turns trying to access the seed, but without success. Suddenly every bird rises in panic as the dark shadow of a hawk crosses the verandah.

Some months after losing our spaniel we adopt Tilly, a bouncy, ball-crazy Airedale terrier. With her curly wool coat and brown button nose she is a cross between a sheep and a teddy bear. Along the far side of the orchard our previous neighbour erected a metal fence, 'to keep out the snakes'. Occasionally Tilly escapes from the back garden and then she heads directly for this fence. Two little fox terriers live on the other side. Although Tilly can hear them, she's never actually seen them. There are several small depressions in the ground underneath the fence where they poke their noses. Tilly doesn't know at which hole a nose will appear, so she waits for a while, quivering in anticipation. When one suddenly pops out, there's barking and a crazy rushing up and down on both sides.

Nearest to the road on the unfenced side of the neighbour's house, there's a small patch of bright green lawn. In the early evening, the whole mob of eleven kangaroos squeezes onto this little square to enjoy the tender green shoots. The neighbour's main windows don't face in this direction so I doubt if he's seen them. In any case, he'll never need to buy a lawnmower.

When she isn't visiting the foxies, Tilly loves to play with soft toys, especially ones which make a noise. At Christmas I buy a toy parrot for my grandchildren. When squeezed, it plays 'Deck the halls with boughs of holly', followed by a raucous squawk. They don't seem very interested in it, but Tilly is. She keeps eyeing it, and when Christmas is almost over she steals it and runs off into the garden. It's buried somewhere, but periodically she digs it up. It is annoying to be woken in the early morning by the sound of Christmas carols, but before we can take the parrot off her, it vanishes again.

Denied adequate winter rainfall, the dams are less than half full at the start of the season. Evaporation soon takes its toll. Already the reduction in soil moisture is resulting in damage to the fruit and a greater vulnerability to disease. Last year's generous error by the water company was all that saved the trees from dying and drastic measures are required if they are to survive another year.

We no longer have enough water to keep everything alive, so I have to make the decision to stop irrigating the native flowers and abandon the project. There are twenty plum trees at the top of the paddock which may also have to be let go. Right now they are in poor condition, mainly because the kangaroos attacked them at the end of summer when there was nothing else to eat.

Recently we have been entertained by boxing matches between the young male roos. Unfortunately, this year one lone vandal has discovered plum trees are springy, making them an ideal alternative when no sparring partner is available. He's doing a lot of damage.

When we planted the young apple trees, we took care to leave a wide margin between them and the roots of the gum trees growing on two sides of the orchard. The drought has continued for so long that even these native trees are struggling for survival, and now new roots reach across the divide for a share of the irrigation water. They are easy to find, for they have scarcely penetrated the surface of the rock-hard ground and I am able to chop them back with an axe.

Before he began his own business, Nick was the engineer at a hospital surrounded by extensive native gardens. The stormwater pipes there were frequently blocked by tree roots. One river red gum put out a root over a hundred metres long, which went straight as an arrow to a water pipe in the distance. I wonder how trees sense the water, especially when it's far away and sealed in a pipe.

It's late summer and in the scorching heat a flock of pink and grey galahs circle overhead before dropping down to drink from the bowl of water I leave for them in the orchard. They scavenge for seed, and when they've gone I see the dusty ground is riddled with holes where they have turned over the soil.

An hour later the sky darkens and a brisk breeze stirs the gum trees. There is a sudden crack of thunder and at long last it begins to rain. As I watch the drops fall, I notice a galah hanging upside down from a branch high above my head. It looks very strange and I'm concerned it may be caught up in something. In a moment though, amid cries of joy, the whole flock is swinging by its feet in the rain.

Two days after this first break in the weather our galahs are back at the nesting box. I wonder why they should be there out of season, but then one bird quickly releases the catch and opens the inspection door. She reaches into the box and emerges with a sprig of gum leaves in her beak. The box gets a thorough cleaning and will be ready for fresh eggs in the spring.

Encouraged by the rainfall, I decide to order next season's fertiliser and perform a soil test. As I zigzag through the orchard collecting earth from twenty holes, I delight in seeing the dark, friable soil, so different from the pale heavy clay of a few years ago. The application of all that lime and good organic matter has had its effect.

A few days later the test results arrive and at first seem encouraging. Then I am shocked to see the salt level in the orchard is sky high. It has never been a problem before. Perhaps it came in with the irrigation water. Even so, a few good storms might have leached it out of the soil. A friend who is an agronomist warns me that any further increase will probably kill the trees.

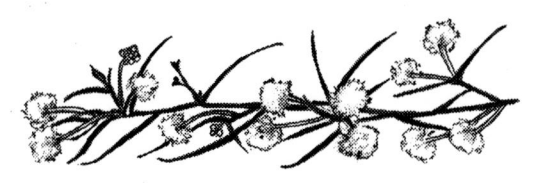

Now the season has ended and the autumn rains have come. Not heavy dam-filling rain, but frequent sweet showers which change the brown dust between the rows into paths of rich green clover. Gum trees that were turning pale and sickly towards the end of summer regenerate new growth, and soon the bush is regaled with the yellow beauty of the wattle. Although there is only one partially filled dam so far, I have new hope for the coming season.

Then I hear that despite the better rainfall, the water in the catchments is at its lowest level ever, so there will be restrictions once again. Without good summer storms, thirty per cent of our allocation will not be enough to keep the trees alive through another year. Soon a letter arrives from the water authority, telling us we will receive no allocation at all this season unless there are massive inflows into the dams in the next few weeks.

It is September and there has been no more rain. Next week a contractor is coming to pull out the trees.

The lame duck and the one-eyed magpie still come to the birdbath. At twilight the kangaroos meet in the front paddock to eat lucerne and drink from the trough. There is enough water to keep a few trees alive, so my grandchildren will know the taste of a Bramley's Seedling, a Cornish Aromatic, and an Autumn Pearmain.

And I have my memories.

Acknowledgements

At times the orchard demanded arduous labour in extremely hot weather. I'm grateful to Les Parslow for coming to work with me whenever I needed him, and for his endless patience. Richard May provided invaluable advice on soil management. My son, Nathaniel, lent a hand when he was home, and my husband always came to my rescue when everything went wrong. I'd like to thank Denise Gadd, gardening guru, and Stephen Ryan, former host of ABC TV's *Gardening Australia*, for their generous comments, and my wonderful editor, Julia Beaven, for her persistence and support. Finally, I owe much to Margaret and Clive Winmill: Margaret for her helpful suggestions and review of the book, and Clive for teaching me almost all I know about apple trees.

Recipe Index

Appelflappen	70
Apple Chutney	54
Apple Dumplings	79
Apple Sauce	56
Bacon and Apple Slice	78
Baked Apples	77
Coffee Hazelnut Cake	104
Cold Tea Cake	44
Dutch Apple Cake	102
Dutch Honey Cake	45
English Sherry Trifle	101
Oliebollen	69
Olive and Tuna Tart	14
Orange Pistachio Biscuits	13
Quince Paste	12
Raw Herring Salad	109
Red Cabbage with Apple	55
Witlof and Anchovy Salad	110

Wakefield Press is an independent publishing and
distribution company based in Adelaide, South Australia.
We love good stories and publish beautiful books.
To see our full range of titles, please visit our website at
www.wakefieldpress.com.au.